ANALYZE IT!

*A fun and easy introduction to software analysis
and the information technology industry*

by Kristen Elliott

Introduction

Hello, reader, it's nice to meet you! I look forward to working with you as you read through **Analyze It!** *A fun and easy introduction to software analysis and the information technology industry.*

Growing up, I had the opportunity to learn a lot of various topics in school, but technology was not necessarily one of them. As a "middle-of-the-road" millennial, I was living between the moments of my parents getting dial-up internet for the first time and buying my first smartphone in college (If you can believe it, I had a flip phone for the entirety of my childhood, and didn't get a smartphone until my sophomore year of undergrad!).

Technology was growing quickly as a field of interest, but not so fast that it was seriously considered when thinking about future career development. As a result, I didn't become acquainted with technology terms, roles, and responsibilities until much later in my education. By the time I joined the workforce, the growth of digital changes and software delivery became much more significant in everyone's lives, so I had a lot of things to learn quickly!

As a technology professional, when I look back at my education, I wish I had a helpful guide that could have introduced software analysis and delivery in a simple way. A lot of times when I talk with my students and friends who aren't in a technology-based career, I often hear sayings like, "It's too complicated," or the mindsets that, "I don't want to," or "I can't code, so it's not for me." I believe the root cause of this problem is majorly due to a lack of awareness of the foundations of technology, which then drives people to think that technology is just too complex. After spending several years in various technology analysis and consulting positions and formally teaching students at the undergraduate level, I can tell you this — understanding the foundations of software analysis and delivery is easy. What's hard sometimes is explaining it in a simple and fun way for everyone to understand.

So that's my promise to you! I promise that I will introduce you to some of the basic concepts of technology and software analysis through a fun and engaging platform. By the end of this book, my hope is that not only will you walk away knowing how to "talk the talk" in software lingo, but you will become potentially interested in exploring a technology career yourself, as well.

Three caveats I want to provide:
1. The purpose of this book is to act as an introduction to the analysis and consulting perspective of technology. I do not have a background in coding; however, there are numerous materials out there to learn the basics of programming. I highly encourage and support you in checking out some the recommended material at the back of the book as a starting point if you want to learn more.
2. I am a firm believer that business and technology go hand-in-hand and create extreme synergies when both parties work together. As a result, this book will focus on both technology-based concepts, as well as some basic business concepts.
3. You may reach the end of this book and realize that this field this isn't for you. If that happens, I want you

to know that there's no shame in that, and you should feel proud for identifying this. I believe a major part of education is finding out what you like or don't like, and I hope that this can serve as a tool for you to continue on that journey.

With that, I hope you enjoy, and read on!

Best,
Kristen

Character summaries:

1. **Marla:** The main character of the story. She is the president of the School Spirit Club and is focused on raising enough money for her entire 8th grade class to go to Happy Amusement Park on the last day of school.
2. **Peter:** Marla's best friend and VP of the School Spirit Club, he supports Marla's efforts.
3. **Mrs. Evans:** A teacher at Riverwood Middle School that sponsors and oversees the School Spirit Club.
4. **Mr. Martinez:** Owner of the school store at Riverwood Middle School.
5. **Mrs. Thompson:** A teacher at Riverwood Middle School that sponsors and oversees the school's Technology Club.
6. **Tamika:** A student within the Technology Club. She acts as a lead analyst in helping the School Spirit Club work with technology to solve their identified problem.
7. **Madeline:** A student within the Technology Club. She supports Tamika as an analyst within the Technology Club.

How this book will read:

Every chapter will be broken into three parts:

1. **Story text:** The story of how the School Spirit Club navigates through an identified problem and how technology can help solve for it.
2. **Guiding and activity questions:** Guiding thoughts and questions for you to think about and discuss with your peers at the end of each story text section.
3. **Key terms review:** A glossary of terms with definitions that are highlighted throughout the story text.

CHAPTER 1 — NO AMUSEMENT PARK TRIP? I AM NOT AMUSED!

Peter: "Hey, check out the falling snow!"

Narrator: Peter points out the window as he and his best friend, Marla, walk through the halls of Riverwood Middle School. Marla looks out the window and shivers in excitement, holding her backpack a little closer. Even though the snow looks beautiful, she knows that with every winter storm, spring is coming closer. Spring is Marla's favorite season for several reasons. She loves the warmer weather and blooming flowers that appear annually, but she also loves the excitement that always comes with the end of the school year. Any projects she works on always finish in the spring, and it is always fun for her to see the positive results of her efforts.

Marla: "It's quite pretty, but we can't stop too long to look at it,

Peter. We're going to be late for Club!"

Narrator: The end-of-school bell rings, and the two of them have about five minutes to get to their favorite after school function, the School Spirit Club. The two of them quickly walk down the chilly hallway to classroom 103 to begin their meeting.

The School Spirit Club is a popular organization at Riverwood Middle School. Typically run by 8th graders, the club's **mission statement** focuses on improving the overall spirit of the school, especially for those in 8th grade, as it's the last grade before high school. The Club puts together two major programs every year to support the improvement of school spirit: the quarterly pep rallies and the end-of-year 8th grade class field trip to Happy Amusement Park. This field trip has been an annual tradition at Riverwood Middle School for the last ten years, and new students entering the school always talk about how amazing the field trip is. All the 8th graders, on the last day of school in May, get up really early in the morning and drive together in luxury buses to the park. Once they get there, they spend the entire day at the park with unlimited ride access. It's often a huge motivation for the students, as it's a memorable event to end their time in middle school.

Marla, as the president of the School Spirit Club, is extremely excited to go on this trip, and she has assumed a lot of responsibilities for planning the event. She is just starting to work with Peter, their Vice President, and their club sponsor, Mrs. Evans, to begin planning for this year's program.

Mrs. Evans greets Marla and Peter as they walk through the door of the classroom. The two are greeted by the other students in Club, as well, as they are preparing to start their meeting. Both of them are in a good mood, considering that other than being cold, they are about to work through the starting details of the trip. The two take their seats and wait for Mrs. Evans to start the meeting. Minutes pass as she goes through roll call and starts administrative topics. When she finally gets to the field trip on her agenda, both Marla and Peter's ears perk up in excitement.

Mrs. Evans: "OK, so I know a lot of you are excited about the annual field trip, right?"

Narrator: She is answered with a resounding "YES" across the classroom.

Mrs. Evans: "Marla created a proposal for the event, so let's give her a few minutes to talk about it."

Narrator: Mrs. Evans looks at Marla for her to begin. Marla quickly gets out her laptop to share her screen with her teammates. Once the document appears, she begins rattling through some of the starting facts and figures.

Marla: "Everyone, this is the current proposed overview of the field trip. Let's start with a few basics — the trip is currently planned for Friday, May 30, which is exactly three months away from today. Like past years, we will go to Happy Amusement Park, which is approximately one hour away from school. We have 140 8th grade students that are expecting to attend this trip."

Mrs. Evans: "Do you happen to know what the current cost per student is that we'll need to account for in our fundraising **budget**?"

Marla: "Yes! I pulled the numbers from Happy Amusement Park's website and learned that thanks to a bulk ticket purchase at our numbers, it will be $40 per person to access the park with unlimited ride access for the entire day."

Mrs. Evans: "Wonderful! That doesn't seem like too much of a price increase from last year. What about transportation and gas? Do you have a projected cost?"

Marla: "Yes, I do! The bus rental is a flat charge of $750 per bus. We will need three buses since each bus carries a max of 50 people. The good news is that the flat charge includes gas and idle time, so there will not be an additional cost for that."

Mrs. Evans: "Excellent. Any other potential costs you can think of?"

Marla: "Well, there were a couple additional things I was thinking of. First off, I imagine there will be a few teachers attending that we will need to account for. How many teachers do you think will attend as chaperones, Mrs. Evans?"

Mrs. Evans: "Great question. In past years, we have had one teacher for every twenty students. So, if you do that math, we will need seven teachers including myself."

Marla: "OK, that's good to know. Two additional things I was thinking of were food and locker rentals. In past years, we have communicated to students that they have to pay for meals and locker rentals out of their own pockets. Should we make that true again for this year?"

Mrs. Evans: "I think so. That's an assumption we have made for the past few years, and I think it's acceptable for us to continue to do so. We usually tell parents in the parent signature form that they should expect to have students bring at least $30 for food, $5 for a locker rental, and $15 for any souvenirs."

Marla: "OK, great. I think that's it then. With those assumptions, this is the **cost plan** I put together, as well as a projected estimate on what we'll need to fundraise."

Narrator: Marla flips to her second page to showcase the plan:

Admission for students (140 tickets at $40 per ticket)	$5,600.00
Admission for teachers (7 tickets at $40 per ticket)	$280.00
Transportation (3 buses at $750 per bus)	$2,250.00
Total estimate	$8,130.00

Mrs. Evans: "This looks great, Marla! Well done."

Narrator: Marla smiles and unplugs her laptop to sit back down at her desk. The other students murmur with excitement.

Mrs. Evans: "Now that we know our expected **cost plan**, let's talk about how we are going to get that money so that our 8th grade class can go!"

Narrator: Mrs. Evans gets up and proceeds to plug in her laptop.

Mrs. Evans: "As everyone knows, this school trip is 100% funded through **fundraising** opportunities performed during the year. In the past, we have gotten the majority of these funds from the school store, which is overseen by Mr. Martinez. We have also gotten funds from other ways, including the annual winter bake sale in January, as well as the annual book festival in October. I pulled our current numbers from so far this year, as well as the numbers from the last two years to show how we're doing. In comparison, we should be at about 75% of our goal by now."

Narrator: Mrs. Evans proceeds to show the year-by-year comparison:

	Two Years Ago	Last Year	Current Year
School Store	$2,829.50	$3,523.30	$1,473.00
Bake Sale	$1,400.00	$1,601.50	$1,650.40
Book Festival	$1,429.50	$1,281.20	$1,568.60
Total	$5,659.00	$6,406.00	$4,692.00
Comparison to goal	$5,659/$7,860 (72%)	$6,406/$8,320 (77%)	$4,692/$8,130 (58)

Peter: "Mrs. Evans, something doesn't look right. With these numbers, it looks like we are far behind if we are supposed to be at 75% of our goal at this point in the year."

Mrs. Evans: "Hmm, you're right. Can anyone tell what looks different about this year?"

Narrator: Everyone takes a moment and looks at the comparison chart. Marla furrows her eyebrows and starts looking line by line, trying to figure out what's different. After a moment, it clicks.

Marla: "I think I know. Is it just me, or does the school store seem to be pulling in less money than in past years?"

Peter: "Yeah, I think you're right! In past years, it looks like it accounts for about 50% of the fundraising goal, but right now it looks to only make up about a third."

Mrs. Evans: "You're absolutely right, you two. This isn't good, as the school store is our main source of fundraising revenue to fund this trip."

Marla: "What does this mean?"

Mrs. Evans: "Well, if we can't get sales increased in the school store, then unfortunately we may be at risk of not being able to fund the trip. We either need to find a different fundraising source or figure out how to help the store."

Peter: "What happens if we can't fix either of those?"

Mrs. Evans: "Well, unfortunately if we can't solve for it, I'm not sure if we'll be able to host the trip this year, team. This has always been a fundraising trip, and our school doesn't have the budget to pay the cost out of its own pocket."

Narrator: The club members start to worry. No annual trip to Happy Amusement Park? Could this be real? Marla wonders what they are going to do!

Chapter One Guiding and Activity Questions:
1. *What do you think is the biggest problem that the School Spirit Club is trying to solve?*
2. *What do you think the Club should do next after discovering their problem?*

Chapter One Key Terms Review:
- **Budget:** An estimate of money coming in and out for a set period of time.
- **Cost plan:** A proposed look of potential costs expected in a project.
- **Fundraising:** The act of seeking financial support for a particular reason.
- **Mission statement:** A brief expression of what an organization's overall goal is, what kind of goods or services the organization offers, and why the organization exists.

CHAPTER 2 — LET'S GET DOWN TO BUSINESS (AND WHAT'S WRONG WITH IT).

As we learned in the previous chapter, the School Spirit Club has identified a major discrepancy: there is a large gap between what they expected the school store to have raised by this point in the year and what it actually has raised. A big question we have to ask is: Why is the school store failing to meet its goal?

Narrator: Marla continues to worry as chatter from the other students fills the room. Not being able to go on the trip after imagining it ever since she walked through the doors of the school on the first day of 6th grade? She has always imagined that day being such a memorable event, one where she and Peter would ride roller coasters again and again until one of them would either puke or faint.

Peter: "Well, how can we solve this? I've been looking forward to going on this trip for three years now, and I'd really like to try make it a reality if possible!"

Narrator: Other students chirp in with a, "Me too!" and "Same!" The consensus in the room is the same — the School Spirit Club's number one goal is to figure out how to fix this.

Mrs. Evans: "Well, I think the first thing we need to figure out is the **root cause** of why the school store isn't bringing in enough **revenue**."

Marla: "What do you mean by "**root cause**," Mrs. Evans?"

Mrs. Evans: "That's a great question, Marla. **Root cause** essentially means we need to understand what the real problem is behind all the current symptoms. For example, I had a student this morning who was late to homeroom. Why do you think that student may have been late?"

Narrator: The students in the Club start thinking about why the student could have been late. No one answers since there are a lot of reasons to be late, and they aren't sure what the correct answer is.

Mrs. Evans: "I'll start us off here — the student was late because they missed their bus. Why do you think they missed their bus?"

Marla: "Was it because they overslept?"

Mrs. Evans: "Yes, exactly. Now let's think, why did the student oversleep?"

Peter: "Oh! They could have overslept because they missed their alarm."

Mrs. Evans: "You're correct! Now, why do you think they missed hearing their alarm?"

Narrator: This question gives the students pause. *Why would a student miss their alarm?*

Marla: "Well, there could be many reasons. They could have not heard it, or forgot to set it, or the alarm stopped working."

Mrs. Evans: "Great callouts. This is something you would obviously have to ask the student. In this particular scenario, it was because they use their phone as an alarm and forgot to charge it overnight, causing them to not wake up on time. So now let's think back here — the original problem is that they were late to class. Everything we listed before understanding that their phone wasn't charged are what we would identify as symptoms of the problem. However, the fact that the phone wasn't charged is the **root cause** of the issue. Does that make sense?"

Narrator: The students start to agree. That does make sense!

Peter: "Yes, it totally does. So, are you suggesting that we can apply this way of thinking to figure out why the school store isn't performing well?"

Mrs. Evans: "Yes, exactly. We call this type of questioning the

"**Five Whys.**" Why? Because typically if you ask "why" five times after a response, that will allow you to get deep enough to understand what the real reason or issue is for a problem."

Marla: "Ah, that makes complete sense! So, who would be the best person for us to start asking these questions to?"

Mrs. Evans: "Well, who do you think would be a good person to start with, Marla?"

Marla: "Hmm...well, I'd say probably Mr. Martinez would be the best person to work with because he oversees the school store.

Mrs. Evans: "I agree! Why don't I go see if he's available for us to **interview** for a few minutes?"

Narrator: Mrs. Evans quickly leaves the room and the students start talking amongst themselves while waiting for her return. A few minutes pass and eventually Mrs. Evans comes back with Mr. Martinez shortly behind.

Mrs. Evans: "Mr. Martinez, thanks again for joining us for a few minutes so that we can ask you a few questions about the school store."

Mr. Martinez: "Of course! "I'm happy to answer any questions you have."

Mrs. Evans: "Excellent. I'll go ahead and kick us off and then, students, feel free to interject. Mr. Martinez, we were looking at the numbers of the school store and noticed that the **revenue** of the store is about 20% less than in past years. Do you think you know why this is happening?"

Mr. Martinez: "That's a great question, Mrs. Evans. I've been wondering that myself, and I think one leading problem is that we just aren't getting a lot of people coming into the store like we used to."

Peter: "Mr. Martinez, in the past, when did students most often come and buy things at the store?"

Mr. Martinez: "Usually after school or during lunch."

Marla: "What kinds of things does the school store sell?"

Mr. Martinez: "Well, in the past we sold school supplies like pencils, folders, highlighters, notebooks, and other things like that. In the past couple of years, we also have started selling apparel like school shirts and jackets, as well as some entertainment support items like headphones and phone chargers."

Marla: "What are your most popular items in the store?"

Mr. Martinez: "I'd say our phone chargers and headphones. Students forget or break those pretty often, so we get a high majority of sales from those items. Beyond that, we get a lot of snack sales after school and a lot of shirt sales when we have upcoming sports games or pep rallies."

Marla: "So do you know why students aren't coming in like they used to?"

Mr. Martinez: "Well, I'm not sure exactly why, but I've noticed that a lot of students who do come in don't end up leaving the store with anything. I started asking them why and it's mostly because they don't have cash on them."

Peter: "Why is that important?"

Mr. Martinez: "Well, the store currently only accepts cash as payment for the goods that we sell."

Peter: "Ah, that makes sense. Why can you only accept cash?"

Mr. Martinez: "It's a limitation of the way we do business in the store. We just have a cashbox. Students have asked me in the past if I can take a credit card or direct payment through one of those third-party applications, but we just don't have the setup today to do that. Honestly, I feel like ever since that popular payment app, Ca$hNow, came out last year, I get asked almost every day if I can accept payment through it.

Peter: OK cool, another follow-up — is going into the store the only way you can buy items?"

Mr. Martinez: "Yeah, unfortunately. I'd love to do a delivery service, but we tried it in the past with order forms and it proved more troublesome than valuable. The students would have to come into the store anyway and pay cash ahead of time. So, we stopped doing order forms and just continue to do in-store purchases only."

Narrator: Marla and Peter both nod in agreement. They suspect that the store's cash-only experience is most likely the **root cause** of the school store's problem.

Mrs. Evans: "Any other questions for Mr. Martinez at this time?"

Narrator: The Club students shake their heads and thank Mr. Martinez for his time. Mr. Martinez smiles, responds with an, "Anytime!," and heads out the door.

Mrs. Evans: "OK, team, so after that interview, I think we all may have a pretty good idea as to why the school store is dealing with this revenue issue, right?"

Peter: "Yeah, it seems that due to an increase in students using cash payment apps like Ca\$hNow, the school store has been impacted because they haven't been able to accommodate payments through the app."

Mrs. Evans: "Agreed. It sounds like the school store's **customers'** preferences have changed, and that's why there's this gap in **revenue**. I think this sounds like a great opportunity for us to build a **persona** of the typical customer for the school store, don't you think? **Peter:** "What's a **persona**?"

Mrs. Evans: "A **persona** is a narrative of a customer's needs and/or preferences. When identifying a problem or building a solution for a person, it's always a good idea to describe who you're trying to solve for. We can make multiple personas for different types of customers, but for now, let's define what we see as the average customer for the school store today."

Marla: "OK, that makes sense" So a typical customer would obviously be someone who goes to this school."

Peter: "Right, and it sounds like a typical customer buys entertainment and snack items, and sometimes apparel for certain occasions throughout the year."

Marla: "Yes, and now it sounds like the customer would prefer a cashless experience when interacting with the store. If they don't have cash in the current environment, that would cause a delay or loss in sale to the store."

Mrs. Evans: "All great points. So, if we put that all together, then I believe we have our key customer **persona**."

Narrator: Mrs. Evans walks to the whiteboard and starts writing down a statement. Once done, she reads it out loud.

Mrs. Evans: "Customer A is a current attendee of Riverwood Middle School. She goes to the school store when she is hungry or needs an electronic item because something broke or was forgotten at home. Sometimes she purchases school clothes when planning to attend a sports or spirit event. She prefers a cashless experience when interacting with the store because she doesn't normally carry cash."

Narrator: The students start to agree. This makes sense based on what Mr. Martinez explained a few minutes ago.

Peter: "So what do we do with this information, Mrs. Evans?"

Mrs. Evans: "Well, I think what's first is to **validate** that this **persona** is real. And once we validate that it's real, we should start to figure out how to meet that persona's needs. Team, I'm going to give you some homework. Since we're meeting again tomorrow, I want each of you to **survey** five of your friends to see if they fit this persona during classes and breaks tomorrow. There are ten of you, so we should be able to get a pretty good **sample size** to validate.

Marla: "I think we can do that! What kind of questions should we ask?"

Mrs. Evans: "Good question! I think you should definitely ask your friends if they have cash on them, and if they use a cash app like Ca$hNow. There are two questions right there. Anything else we should ask?"

Marla: "Hmm, well it may be good to see what types of items they have purchased in the past at the store."

Peter: "Oh, and how often they visit the store now?"

Mrs. Evans: "Yes, those are good questions to ask! Anything else?"

Peter: "Well, is it OK to ask them if the school store became a cashless experience, would they be interested in buying more things from the store?"

Mrs. Evans: "Yes, I think that's completely OK to ask. That would help us understand the **desirability** of the change. And if students respond saying that they wouldn't go to the store if it changed its payment policy, then that isn't the **root cause** of the problem."

Peter: "Agreed, that makes sense."

Mrs. Evans: "OK, so let's write these questions down, everyone, and then when you're asking your friends, record their responses on a sheet of paper or your laptops, please."

Narrator: Mrs. Evans goes to the board and writes the following questions:

1. *Do you have cash on you today? (Yes/No)*
2. *Do you use any cash payment apps (like Ca$hNow)? (Yes/No)*
    1. *If yes, what do you use? (This will be a different response per student.)*
3. *How often have you gone to the school store in the past? (Never, daily, weekly, monthly, quarterly, once a year)*
4. *What have you normally bought at the store in the past? (This will be a different response per student.)*
5. *If the school store allowed non-cash payment options, do you think you would go to the store more? (Yes/No)*
6. *If the school store offered homeroom delivery, do you think you would go to the store more? (Yes/No)*

Mrs. Evans: "Team, does this look good to you?"

Marla and Peter: "Yes!"

Narrator: Everyone in the Club responds in unison alongside Marla and Peter. Marla sighs a breath of relief. It feels to her that they now have some sort of plan in place to analyze this problem. She looks forward to asking a few of her friends tomorrow and figuring out if their analysis is correct!

Chapter Two Guiding and Activity Questions:

1. Besides asking "Why" questions to a person in an interview, what other types of questions can you ask?

2. Work with a partner or a small group to identify a problem that you or a friend is dealing with in school. Can you understand the root cause of that problem using the Five Whys technique? Be prepared to explain how you got to your root cause.

3. Take an example of a major business (examples: McDonalds, Amazon, Target, etc.) and create one persona that you think would fit their business model.

4. Take a look again at the survey questions that the School Spirit Club put together. Are there any additional questions you think you would ask if you were in the club?

Chapter Two Key Terms:

- **Customer**: A person that buys goods or services from a business.

- **Desirability**: The understanding of whether or not a solution meets the wants and needs of your users.

- **Five Whys**: An analysis technique that allows a person to explore the cause and effect relationships of a situation to identify an underlying problem.

- **Interview**: A discussion with one or multiple people to learn about something.

- **Persona**: A perceived representation of a person's or group of people's characteristics.

- **Root cause**: The reason that a problem exists.
- **Revenue**: Money coming in from an organization's sales of goods or services.

- **Sample size**: Number of people included in a survey research effort.

- **Survey**: To conduct research with any number of individuals to discover and/or validate information.
- **Validate** - To check that something is correct.

CHAPTER 3 — PROBLEM HAS BEEN ANALYZED! NOW, WHAT ABOUT A SOLUTION...?

Now that the School Spirit Club has identified a potential reason as to why the school store is failing to meet its goal, the club members are actively trying to validate their hypothesis. If confirmed, what should the next steps of the Club members be to proceed?

Narrator: Time moved quickly for the school spirit club members, and before anyone knew it, the next day had already rolled around. Marla and Peter enter classroom 103, getting ready to present their findings from the questions they asked their friends in hopes to validate and confirm that their **problem statement** is correct.

Mrs. Evans: "Good afternoon, everyone! Are we ready to share our survey results?"

Narrator: The team nods and starts pulling out their laptops, where they recorded their findings.

Mrs. Evans: "Excellent! If you can, let's go through these questions one by one."

Narrator: The team begins to process each question, and before they know it, they have completed their exercise The results are shown on the whiteboard:

Question	Majority Responses
Do you have cash on you today? (Yes/No)	No (70%)
Do you use any cash payment apps (like Ca$hNow)? (Yes/No) If yes, what do you use? (This will be a different response per student.)	Yes (85%) All students who answered "yes" named Ca $hNow as their payment application.

How often have you gone to the school store in the past? (Never, daily, weekly, monthly, quarterly, once a year)	Monthly (50%); never (20%); quarterly (10%); weekly (5%); daily (5%); once a year (10%)
What have you normally bought at the store in the past? (This will be a different response per student.)	Different responses, but the majority of people said cell phone chargers, earphones, Chapstick, gum, T-shirts, and snacks.
If the school store allowed non-cash payment options, do you think you would go to the store more? (Yes/No)	Yes (95%)
If the school store offered home-room delivery, do you think you would go to the store more? (Yes/No)	Yes (80%)

Mrs. Evans: "Now this is what I call good research! Out of our sample size surveyed, I think we can make a confident statement that not only is the persona we wrote yesterday correct, but Mr. Martinez did help us identify the root cause of the school store's problem. We need to find a way to solve its payment issue in order to bring more students into the store."

Narrator: The students agree throughout the classroom. Excited, Peter speaks up and asks the next question.

Peter: "So now that we know what the problem is, how can we solve for it?"

Mrs. Evans: "Great question, Peter. I think this is a perfect time for all of us to try **brainstorming**. Does everyone know what brainstorming is?"

Narrator: Some students nod while others shake their heads.

Mrs. Evans: "That's OK! **Brainstorming** is when we take time to create a bunch of ideas that may solve the problem that we have identified. There is no wrong way to brainstorm, but there are a couple rules that we'll want to follow."

Narrator: Mrs. Evans stands up to further accentuate her position.

Mrs. Evans:

- "Rule number one: In this classroom, we do not brainstorm alone. Brainstorming is all about people and collaboration of ideas!
- Rule number two: There is no bad idea; therefore, you are not allowed to judge an idea that someone says. You must write it down. Even if you think it's a wild idea, encourage it!
- Rule number three: When we brainstorm, we will have a time limit so that we do not get too frustrated or start repeating ideas. And finally,
- Rule number four: In this classroom, everyone has to participate with a smile and energy! It's never fun when you have someone who doesn't want to participate.

Following those rules, let's take thirty minutes and get into groups of four to brainstorm. How does that sound?"

Narrator: Everyone agrees in excitement and starts to formulate groups. Marla quickly grabs Peter to join her team, as well as a couple of other close friends. Mrs. Evans' timer starts and they began to **ideate**.

Narrator: Thirty minutes later, Mrs. Evans's timer starts buzzing, which indicates the end of everyone's brainstorming sessions. She signals for everyone to return to their desks, and once everyone is seated she has a representative come up and write all of their ideas on the board. A few more minutes pass, and then the board holds a list of everyone's ideas to solve the problem:

1. *Get Mr. Martinez a register where he can accept credit cards*
2. *Have Mr. Martinez do a post-purchase payment if someone forgets cash (IOUs)*
3. *Advertise certain items in the weekly newspaper to interest more students to come to the school store*
4. *Build a phone app for the school store that can take electronic payments*

There are many other statements on the board, but all of them echo one of these four recommendations, so these are circled.

Mrs. Evans: "These are some great ideas, everyone. They are all diverse solutions, and I can tell everyone really got into the exercise and came up with some potentially great options to consider."

Marla: "So, what do we do now?"

Mrs. Evans: "Well, I think as a group we should discuss each suggestion and vote on which one we'd like to try out. It's important to note at this point that whatever option we choose, we should prepare to pivot and change paths if we determine at any point that it's not **feasible**. This type of mindset is what we call **"Fail Fast, Learn Quickly."** It's completely OK to fail as long as we learn something from it. Does that make sense?"

Narrator: The students nod their heads and begin to think about which option would be best to start with.

Mrs. Evans: "So, let's start with idea number one. What positives and what challenges do you think we would encounter with this option?"

Peter: "Well, I think the immediate benefit is that the school store would have a different payment option besides cash. But a challenge I can see is that getting a register with a credit card reader costs money, and Mr. Martinez may not have money available to do that without eating into our fundraising revenue. Additionally, we don't know if everyone has a credit card."

Mrs. Evans: "Great call-outs, Peter. Team, what about idea number two?"

Marla: "Well, going with IOUs would certainly lower the risk of losing sales, but I'm not sure how easy that would be to track and manage IOUs. That could get really challenging and cumbersome."

Mrs. Evans: "Yes, all good points. What about idea number three?"

Peter: "I think this could pair really well with another solution, but I'm not sure if it solves the problem we're talking about, which is the fact that students don't carry cash."

Mrs. Evans: "Great. And finally, what about idea number four?"

Marla: "I really like this idea. I don't know how to code though, so I'm not sure how difficult it would be to do."

Peter: "Yeah, I agree. Does anyone here know how to code?"

Narrator: All the students in the classroom shrug and shake their heads.

Marla: "Well, what about asking the Technology Club? We could see if the members or their teacher can help us out.

Mrs. Evans: "That's a great idea! If we can collaborate with the Technology Club, they might even be able to help us create a **prototype** and test with students.

Peter: "What's a prototype?"

Mrs. Evans: "Great question. A prototype is something you build quickly to get your solution idea across, with the goal being to **test** it with people to determine if it's not only a **desirable,** but also a **feasible** solution for what you're trying to solve. Often you want to think, *what's the quickest way I can get some-*

thing in front of my customer?"

Peter: "Ah, that makes sense. Does our prototype have to even be code-based?"

Mrs. Evans: "No, it can be as simple as a piece of paper as long as it gets our point across. Before we build a prototype however, we need to identify what our **requirements** are. Requirements are basically statements of how we expect a **user** to interact with a system, like the phone app that we're proposing."

Peter: "OK, that makes sense!"

Mrs. Evans: "So team, out of all these options, which one would everyone like to try first?"

Narrator: The students take a moment to discuss amongst themselves. When they've reached a consensus, Marla delivers it aloud.

Marla: "An overwhelming majority of us want to try building the phone app. It seems like a really creative way of solving Mr. Martinez's problem at the school store, and if it works out well, it could be used for years to come! We'd be trendsetters for future grades."

Mrs. Evans: "Wonderful, then I think we have an idea that we want to start building and **prototyping**! I think as a next step, I'll see if Mrs. Thompson and the Technology Club would be interested in joining us at our next club meeting on Thursday. Having them collaborate with us to identify our **requirements** may be very helpful, and can also help us determine quickly if they can assist us in building a phone app. Sound like a plan?"

Narrator: The students agree in excitement and then realize that the Club's meeting time has ended. Mrs. Evans congratulates them on their hard work as the students put away their materials and begin to leave the classroom for the day.

Chapter Three Guiding and Activity Questions:

1. Break up into groups of 4-6 people and continue to brainstorm about the story's problem statemen: The school spirit club needs to find a way to solve the payment issue problem in order to bring more students into the school store.

2.
   a. What other ideas did you come up with? Any technology-based ideas?
   b. Out of your ideas, which do you think is the most desirable? Which do you think is the most feasible?

3. Draw a prototype using a piece of paper and pen for the following scenario: *You are building a website for your school's library and you want to demonstrate how a student can check out a book.*

Chapter Three Key Terms:

- **Brainstorming:** The act of coming up with multiple ideas.

- **Desirable:** The opinion that a solution is wanted by the customer.

- **Fail Fast, Learn Quickly:** Trying an idea without the fear of failing, because if you fail fast you can quickly understand what went wrong and learn from it.

- **Feasible (feasibility):** The idea that a solution can being easily achieved.

- **Ideate:** To come up with an idea.

- **Problem statement:** A brief statement that defines a challenge faced by a business. It's typically seen as a starting point for coming up with a solution, such as a product or technology vision.

- **Prototype**: A quick try at creating a solution based on identified requirements.

- **Requirements**: Things that are needed or wanted.

- **Test:** To make sure that something works. In software terms, it's to check the quality, performance, and/or reliability of a piece of developed software.

- **User:** A person that uses (or will use) a piece of software that has been developed.

CHAPTER 4 — WELCOME, TECHNOLOGY CLUB!

The School Spirit Club has brainstormed and selected a potential solution option to try out. The Club members have identified that collaborating with the Technology Club could help them be successful. But, what exactly is the Technology Club?

Narrator: The following day, the School Spirit Club members prepare themselves to meet the Technology Club. Mrs. Evans has worked with Mrs. Thompson to find a larger room to accommodate everyone, and so all the students from both clubs file into classroom 250 to meet and get to know each other.

Mrs. Evans: "Thanks again for meeting with us. We can't adequately express our appreciation for your willingness to hear our problem statement and interest in how we may be able to collaborate."

Mrs. Thompson: "Of course! I think this is a great real-world example for the kids to try out, and when some of the students heard it was to help support the end of year 8th grade trip, they were very excited and ready to support."

Mrs. Evans: "Wonderful! So, I think the best way to start is for us to introduce ourselves and tell you all a little more about the challenge that we're facing today."

Narrator: Mrs. Evans takes the next few minutes to talk about the School Spirit Club and the issue of meeting their fundraising goal, as well as some of the pre-work they had already done to establish their persona and root cause of the problem. She ends by explaining the group's interest in building a phone application to help fix the problem. The Technology Club sits and listens, taking notes as Mrs. Evans explains. Once Mrs. Evans finishes, Mrs. Thompson gets up and begins her introduction of the Technology Club.

Mrs. Thompson: "Hi, everyone! We are the Technology Club of Riverwood Middle School. We have seven students in this club that have an interest in a technology-based career when they are older, and who are focused on building their **analysis**, **development**, and **testing** skills. We are always looking for real-world scenarios where we can use the power of technology to solve real people's needs, and we think that we can certainly help your club based on the information you've provided."

Mrs. Evans: "That's great! I'm not sure if I completely understand by what you mean **analysis**, **development**, and **testing** though, can you explain those further?"

Mrs. Thompson: "Of course. When we say **analysis** we mean the act of taking a problem or idea and breaking it down to get a better understanding of it. When we say **development**, we mean the act of building a piece of technology through the power of writing code, and when we say **testing**, we mean the act of making sure what we have built actually works. A really big misconception about technology is that a person in the field only codes, but in reality, we try to look at the big picture, see how technology can support it, and then try to buildit. . Does that make sense?"

Mrs. Evans: "Yes, that does! So, does that mean that not every-one in your club codes?"

Mrs. Thompson: "Yes, exactly. Four of our students actively code and the remaining three act as analysts and testers. We try to embody the idea that we are an **Agile build team**, which basically means that we are a "cross-functional" group of people who "define, build, test, and deliver" a piece of technology that gives value to our customer as quickly as we can[1].

Marla: "What do you mean by the term **agile**?"

Mrs. Thompson: "When we say **agile**, we basically mean that we're trying to respond as quickly and as flexibly as possible to a customer's needs. The term **"agile"** means to move quickly and easily, and we strive to do the same in response to needs."

Peter: "This really surprises me. I had the thought that everyone in the Technology Club would be a **developer**."

Mrs. Thompson: "You'd be surprised how often we hear that! Having a technology career is not limited to just **coding**. In fact, there are a wide range of roles needed in technology, such as a **project manager**, a **business analyst**, and a **quality engineer**. Companies will always need people who can understand technology, but they also need people who can understand their business to determine how technology can support their operations.

Mrs. Evans: "So, how do we start working with you and your club?"

Mrs. Thompson: "Well, the first thing I think we need to do is define your software **requirements**. **Requirements** are essentially the things that your users need or want when interacting with the technology. We know that you want to build a proto-type of a mobile app, so it's all about identifying how your user would interact with the mobile app. Our **requirements** lead, Tamika, will work with your team to define all these **require-ments** and write them down for our developers to understand.

After **requirements** are completed, then we can build a first draft of the mobile app through **coding**, which is es-sentially writing instructions in a computer program to per-form a specific task. Developers code through a **programming language** and often use a software **framework** to start. Some examples of programming languages are Java, HTML, and C++. Once **coding** is complete, we can do some **user testing,** and then showcase it to you all to see if we built what you were looking for.

I think to get started as quickly as possible, let's have Tamika work with your team to start the **requirements** session. Tamika, do you want to introduce yourself?"

Tamika: "Hi, everyone, I'm Tamika! As Mrs. Thompson said, I will work with your team to define all of your **requirements** so that we can appropriately turn your needs into code. This will take a little bit of time, but since you already gave us a persona, I think it will be fairly easy to get started. Who can I work with to define the **requirements**?"

Mrs. Evans: "How about Marla and Peter, you work with Tamika for the rest of Club time to get started on the **requirements**?"

Marla: "Sure, we'd be happy to help."

Narrator: Peter nods his head in agreement.

Mrs. Thompson: "Excellent. Tamika, let's include Madeline in the breakout session, as well. She can help support your documentation, and it will give her some exposure to identifying user needs."

Tamika: "Sounds good!"

Narrator: Tamika motions Madeline to follow her out of the room. Marla and Peter follow suit and the four of them go to the

classroom next door to begin their first **requirements** session.

Chapter Four Guiding and Activity Questions:

1. What roles do you think of when you think of technology? Were you surprised by any of the different role examples?

2. Is there a particular role that interests you? On your own or with a partner, do some research about a role you'd like to learn more about.

3. Agile focuses on the mindset of breaking work into smaller increments to create and deliver value to a customer quicker and better. Can you think of an example where doing something in an agile way would be helpful for you?

Chapter Four Key Terms:

-   **Agile**: A key concept in software analysis and development. The ability to move quickly and easily when defining requirements and building a solution.

-   **Agile build team**: A cross-functional group of people who analyze, define, build, test, and deliver a piece of value quickly to their customers through software. Typically 6-10 people work within a team, including analysts, developers, testers, a product owner, and a Scrum Master.

-   **Analysis**: The process of understanding and defining a process or business function in order to identify needs and goals to create systems and procedures that will provide value to the current state.

-   **Coding**: The process of writing instructions within a computer program to accomplish a specific task.

-   **Business analyst**: A person who carefully considers and defines business needs to improve business processes, products, and service functions.

-   **Development**: The process of designing, testing, and

implementing a new piece of software.

- **Developer**: A person who builds software.

- **Framework**: A software structure that a developer can use as a baseline, and then make specific coding changes to reach their programming goal.

- **Project manager**: A person who is in charge of planning and executing a project.

- **Programming language**: A set of rules to tell a computer to perform a set of specific tasks.

- **Requirements**: Things that are needed or wanted.

- **Quality engineer**: A person who makes sure software or procedures in place are of the best quality possible.

- **Testing**: The process of checking quality, performance, and/or reliability of developed software. The terms "Quality Assurance" and "QA testing" are widely used in the software development industry.

- **User testing**: The process of validating the functions of a product or service by a real user to determine if it's working correctly or not.

Chapter Four References:

1. Knaster, Richard. "SAFe 5.0 Framework." Scaled Agile Framework, September 14, 2020. http://www.scaledagileframework.com/.

CHAPTER 5 — LET'S GET TO THE MAIN REQUIREMENTS!

*The School Spirit Club just met with the Technology Club and learned more about who they are and what they can do to work together. The first identified step in their collaboration is to gather their user requirements. What will Marla, Peter, Tamika, and Madeline discover in their first **elicitation** session?*

Narrator: Marla and Peter sit down in classroom 206 with Tamika and Madeline ready to begin their first requirements session. Tamika stands up at the whiteboard while Madeline sits down next to Marla and Peter with her laptop out.

Tamika: "OK, so I think the first thing we need to identify are all the users that you think would use this future application. You all already provided us with a persona that I think fits the user of your customer, which would be a student here at school. Are there any other users you can think of that may interact with this proposed solution?"

Peter: "Well, the only other person I can think of is Mr. Martinez. I guess he would have different needs, right?"

Marla: "Yeah, I think so. A student will be buying things from the store, while Mr. Martinez will need to know what items are being bought in order to fill the orders."

Tamika: "Great callout. We will treat Mr. Martinez as a separate user then, since he is going to need to know when a purchase has been made. What other needs do you think Mr. Martinez will have?"

Marla: "I think that he is going to need to be able to tell the student user when their purchased items are ready for pickup."

Peter: "Yeah, I agree. I also think he probably will want to be able to mark an order as "done," so that he doesn't get confused about whether an order has been completed or not."

Marla: "Yes! I would also imagine that it'd be nice for Mr. Martinez to see a summary of all sales made through the app. That would make it a lot easier to see if the tool has been a valuable addition."

Narrator: Madeline starts jotting down some items on her laptop.

Tamika: "OK, great! Anything else you can think of?"

Marla: "That's all I can think of for Mr. Martinez. Should we move to the student user needs?"

Tamika: "Yes, I think this is enough to start with for Mr. Martinez. Moving on to the student user, I imagine we should consider all potential view and update actions for the user. We use this acronym in analysis called **V.A.E.R**. It stands for View, Add,

Edit, and Remove[2]. Let's start with "view" first. What do you two think the student user should be able to "view?"

Marla: "Well, I think the student will want to obviously view all items that they can purchase. And I imagine if they select an item to view, then they should see some details tied to the item, like how much it is for example."

Peter: "Yeah, I agree. The student should also be able to view all items they've selected to order before buying them to see if they want to make any changes."

Tamika: "OK, great. I think the only other thing I was thinking of for "view" is what about the scenario after the student has added their payment information for purchase and they check out. What happens then?"

Peter: "It would be nice to get a confirmation that the purchase went through. I also imagine that it will take a minute for Mr. Martinez to fill the order, so the student should be able to view a pickup day and time telling them when they can get their items from the store."

Tamika: "That makes sense to me! With that, let's move to "add". What "add" scenarios can you think of?"

Marla: "The only one I can think of is a student selecting or "adding" an item that they want to purchase."

Peter: "Yeah, that's a good callout. What about allowing users to add details about themselves? I imagine it would get kind of redundant to add their personal information every time they want to make a purchase. It would be helpful if they had a profile."

Marla: "Oh yes, definitely. And of course, adding a payment method is important."

Tamika: "Your team mentioned the cash-based application, Ca$hNow, would be a preferred payment method. Any other payment methods that you think a student would want to add?"

Marla: "I have my mom's credit card that she lets me use sometimes, and we know from our survey results that other students have access to credit cards, too, so we should have that as a payment option."

Tamika: "OK, cool that makes a lot of sense."

Narrator: Madeline continues to write some things down on her laptop.

Tamika: "Let's move onto "edit" scenarios."

Marla: "For "edit" scenarios, I think the student should be able to edit anything they identify that they want to buy. For example, if I want to buy two packs of gum, I should be able to edit the selected quantity from one to two packs. Oh, and the student should be able to edit any personal information we ask of them on their profile."

Tamika: "Yeah, that's a good callout. In my mind, we probably just want their name, email address, and phone number for their personal information. Would you two agree with that?"

Narrator: Marla and Peter both agree. Madeline continues to make notes on her laptop.

Marla: "I think that's it for me on "edit" scenarios. For the last of your acronym, "remove," I think the only thing would be that a student should be able to remove a selected item so they don't actually have to buy it if they change their mind,. That's all I can think of, though."

Peter: "Yeah, I think that's it, as well."

Tamika: "Great! Madeline have you been able to keep up on note taking during this conversation?"

Narrator: Madeline nods her head as she begins to wrap up her typing.

Tamika: "For your awareness, Madeline is acting as the **scribe** for this session. The role of the **scribe** is really important in analysis because the main goal of the position is to write down identified user needs and notes from our discussion into clear statements for our coders to review. I've been acting as the **facilitator** for this session, which basically means that I'm asking you a bunch of questions to make sure we understand your user needs."

Narrator: Marla and Peter both smile and nod in understanding.

Madeline: "I think I've got everything! Let me show you my current list of user needs. I always try to put these needs in the perspective of the user, so hopefully these make sense."

Narrator: Madeline proceeds to take her laptop to the front of the room so she can project for others to see.

List of user needs (student):

1. *As a user, I want to be able to view a summary of all available products for sale in the school store so that I can decide*

if I want to buy any.

2. *As a user, I want to be able to view details of a specific product so that I can learn more about the item (details, price, etc.).*
3. *As a user, I want to be able to select one to many products so that I can identify that I want to buy them.*
4. *As a user, I want to be able to remove <one, many, all> product(s) I've previously selected to buy so that I no longer have to buy them if I change my mind.*
5. *As a user, I want to be able to edit the quantity of a selected product so that I can purchase more than one at the same time.*
6. *As a user, I want to have a profile that contains my information so that I don't have to put in my information every time I want to buy something (name, phone #, email).*
7. *As a user, I want to be able to have the option to buy selected product(s) through my cash application profile (Ca$hNow) so that I do NOT have to buy my products with a credit card.*
8. *As a user, I want to be able to have the option to buy selected product(s) with a credit card so that I do NOT have to buy my products with a cash application.*
9. *As a user, I want to receive a confirmation of my purchased product(s) after completion of payment method so that I know that I have successfully bought the product(s) I am interested in.*
10. *As a user, I want to receive a date and time window informing me when I can pick up my purchased product(s) at the school store.*

List of user needs (Mr. Martinez):

1. *As a user, I want to be notified when there has been a purchase of product(s) so that I can pull product(s) off the shelf.*
2. *As a user, I want to be able to notify the buyer when their product(s) are ready for pickup so that I can complete the*

sale.

3. *As a user, I want to be able to mark a transaction as "complete" once the student has picked up their product(s) so that I can complete the sale.*
4. *As a user, I want to be able to see a record of all sales made in one location so that I can see a summary of revenue.*

Tamika: "Madeline, these look great to me. Well done! Marla and Peter, as you can see, every statement follows a pattern from the perspective of the user. We try to follow the mindset that as a specific user, they want or need the ability to do something that provides them value. For us, these needs also become **user stories**, which allow us to communicate our requirements more clearly and quickly to our developers. Does that make sense to you two? Do you see any missing requirements?"

Marla: "No, I think this looks great. What do you think, Peter?"

Peter: "I think all these statements are correct, but it's hard to see if we're missing any scenarios here. Is there anything we can do to make sure we've covered our bases?"

Tamika: "I think this sounds like a great opportunity to create a future state **process map**. We create these a lot to visually chart customer behavior."

Peter: "That sounds like a good idea. I've never created a **process map** before. How do you create one?"

Narrator: Tamika grabs a marker and goes to the whiteboard to begin to draw.

Tamika: "It's simple once you get the hang of it. Since we just have two users, we'll create two horizontal rows to record any activities done by each user. We call these **swimlanes**. After that, we identify the starting point, as well as the ending point, of our story. And then finally, we fill in step-by-step our expectations to get from start to finish. Marla, what do you think is the first thing that needs to happen to start this scenario? What about the last thing?"

Marla: "I think the start of the flow is a student wants to buy something, and the end of the flow is when the student has the item that they've purchased."

Narrator: Tamika draws two placeholder circles on the flow in the student **swimlane**.

Tamika: "OK, great. Now we fill in everything in between, marking the activities that the student or Mr. Martinez has to do to get from the starting point to the ending point."

Narrator: The team starts collaborating at the whiteboard. Twenty minutes pass by and the team finally completes their **process map**:

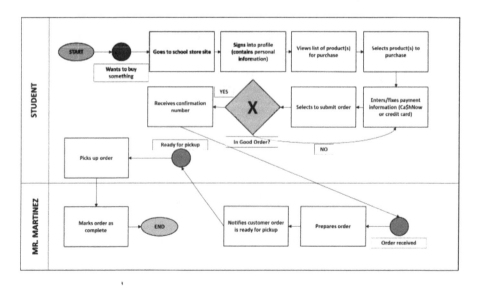

Tamika: "After seeing this process map, do you two see anything missing?

Peter: "For now I don't see anything. This chart is really helpful, and I feel pretty confident we have given you our user needs!"

Tamika: "Wonderful! I think that is enough for our requirements gathering session. In my mind, the next steps are for you two to create a prototype with these defined user needs and validate with Mr. Martinez and a few students that we are going in the right direction. In parallel, we can take these notes back to our developers and have them review the scenarios. If there are any questions, then we will pull you two back in for another session. This will take a little time, but we should hopefully be able to check in with you two and your group in a week."

Marla: "That sounds like a great plan. Thank you so much for helping us out!"

Tamika: "Absolutely!"

Narrator: The four of them, happy with their work, close up their materials and head back to classroom 205 to finish out the day. After sharing the requirements with the larger group and gaining consensus, the afternoon winds down and both groups head out for the day.

Chapter Five Guiding and Activity Questions:

1. Read through the list of user needs again for the two identified personas. Do you think there are any user needs that Marla and Peter missed in their first requirements session with Tamika and Madeline? If yes, what do you think is missing?

2. As we learned in the story, a process map can be used to visually chart out expected customer behavior. Process maps can also be used to represent current state behavior. Work with a partner to complete the following:
   a. List out the current steps you, as a user, would take to read a new email in your inbox. Remember to use V.A.E.R. to help you identify your steps if you get stuck.
   b. Once those steps are identified, try plotting them out in a current state process map. Be prepared to share with your classmates.

3. Now that the group's user needs have been identified, work with your own small group (4-6 people) to create a prototype that you will present to Mr. Martinez and the students in the School Spirit Club. Use only pencil and paper for this exercise.
   a. Note: For your prototype, make sure you focus on major points of the identified user needs. Remember that a prototype should get your point across for a solution and should be easy enough to understand that anyone can read it and provide feedback.

Chapter Five Key Terms:

- **Elicitation**: The act of collecting information. In software analysis, it specifically focuses on gathering information to create requirements.

- **Facilitator**: A person who leads and manages a requirements gathering session with the goal of identifying user needs and requirements.

- **Process map**: A tool that can visually show a step-by-step map of a current or future state process.

- **Scribe**: A person who takes notes during a requirements gathering session with the goal of documenting user needs and requirements.

- **Swimlane**: A visual way in a process map that can show the differences between activities of different users in a process.

- **User stories**: Brief descriptions of the needs of a user. Used to help communicate requirements in building software.

- **V.A.E.R.**: Acronym used to help capture all potential scenarios when gathering requirements. Stands for: View, Add, Edit, Remove.

Chapter Five References:
- 2 – The V.A.E.R. acronym is a fictious term based on the standard term C.R.U.D., which stands for Create, Read, Update, and Delete. More information on CRUD can be found at https://www.codecademy.com/articles/what-is-crud.

CHAPTER 6 —
CHECK-IN TIME!

Marla, Peter, Tamika, and Madeline just finished a very productive requirements elicitation session, and now have a list of defined user needs for students at Riverwood Middle School, as well as for Mr. Martinez as the overseer of the school store. Marla and Peter need to create a prototype and review the identified needs with Mr. Martinez and a few students, while Tamika and Madeline need to begin reviewing the identified needs with their developers. Will these activities prove successful, or will they have to regroup and start from square one?

Narrator: The next few days pass quickly as both groups set out to accomplish their objectives from their previous requirements elicitation session. Marla and Peter start by creating a prototype based on the identified user needs and showing it to Mr. Martinez and a few students within the School Spirit Club. Mr. Martinez is pleasantly surprised with their idea for a solution and becomes very invested in seeing a completed product. Marla and Peter receive similar feedback from their peers within the School Spirit Club. Happy with the feedback, the two communicate the good news back to Tamika and Madeline.

After a couple more days, Tamika reaches back out to Marla and Peter to share their current progress with the developers. Marla is especially excited to hear about progress being made, and she is hopeful that the Technology Club has good news to share. The two clubs agree to meet after school that day, and when 3 p.m. rolls around, they all come together in classroom 205 to start their discussion.

Mrs. Thompson: "Alright, team, why don't we give the School Spirit Club an update on where we are with the requirements and our coding of the prototype? Tamika, why don't you go first?"

Tamika: "Certainly! Last week we had a very productive requirements gathering session with Marla and Peter, and then we were able to showcase our list of features to our developers. There was a follow-up question about one scenario that we'd like to clarify now if that's alright."

Narrator: Tamika motions for Madeline to present her notes on her laptop.

Madeline: "Someone brought up the question about when a student wants to order something and the item is out-of-stock. We have an idea on how we want to address that, but wanted to check with the Club first to see what they expect in user behavior."

Marla: "If I was interacting with the tool, I would want to know immediately if something was out-of-stock, rather than later in the process. Also, I would expect that Mr. Martinez should be able to indicate when an out-of-stock product is now in-stock."

Madeline: "OK, great! I think we are in agreement with that, so I will add two new user needs per those scenarios and update our process flow."

Tamika: "Next, I'd like to review with you our current **business rules** and **non-functional requirements** to make sure you all agree with those statements."

Mrs. Thompson: "Tamika, let's briefly explain what a **business rule** and a **non-functional requirement** are since not everyone might know what those terms mean. Do you want to explain them, or would you like me to?"

Tamika: "I think I can do it! Let's start with **business rules** first. The easiest way I can explain them are as definitions or constraints about the business that you are operating. The word rule plays heavily into a **business rule** because it helps provide some expected logic. Does that make sense?"

Narrator: Members of both clubs nod and agree simultaneously.

Tamika: "OK, great. I'd like to show you the current list of **business rules** we have written per our requirements gathering session and recorded needs. Please read through them and let me know if you disagree with any statements."

Business Rules:
- *A customer must be a student at Riverwood Middle School.*
- *A customer must be associated with one profile in order to buy something.*
- *A customer's profile must be secured with a password.*
- *A customer can only purchase items through either a credit card or a cash app (Ca$hNow).*
- *A customer can buy from one to multiple items in one order (one-to-many relationship).*
- *Mr. Martinez is the only user that can fill and complete orders.*

Tamika: "Oh, and let's add one more now that we have answered the question about out-of-stock items."

Narrator: Madeline quickly types up a new rule for all to see:
- *A customer must be a student at Riverwood Middle School.*
- *A customer must be associated with one profile in order to buy something.*

- *A customer can only purchase items through either a credit card or a cash app (Ca$hNow).*
- *A customer can buy from one to multiple items in one order (one-to-many relationship).*
- *Mr. Martinez is the only user that can fill and complete orders.*
- **A customer cannot purchase an item that is out-of-stock.**

Tamika: "Are there any questions or concerns with the listed business rules?"

Marla: "No, I think these statements make sense to me. Thanks for showing these to us!"

Tamika: "Of course! With that, let's move on to **non-functional requirements**. Now these are going to be more technical statements, as a **non-functional requirement** is a constraint or piece of logic that is tied to the system that we plan to build. I would like to review these with you all, and I can clarify any that do not make sense. As a heads-up, all these statements are generic in saying "system." When we say "system," we are referring to the phone app that we are building."

Narrator: Tamika then proceeds to showcase a new page for everyone to see:

Non-functional Requirements (NFRs):

1. *The system will be available twenty-four hours per day, seven days per week.*
2. *The system will undergo quarterly maintenance changes, resulting in the system being down once a quarter for X period of time.*
3. *The system will require a password per profile with the following requirements: at least eight characters including at least one symbol character.*
4. *The system will require a profile's password to be changed every ninety calendar days.*
5. *The system will be available in the English language.*
6. *The system will provide a response time of X seconds.*
7. *The system will be accessible on iOS or Android.*
8. *The system will be able to manage up to 200 users at a time.*

Tamika: "Are there any questions per these statements?"

Peter: "I have one. I noticed some of these statements have an X called out, like in statement number six. What does that mean?"

Tamika: "Great question. That means that we're not completely sure right now, so we are using a placeholder. We call this the **x-factor**, since we know it will eventually be replaced with a real metric. Because that number is unknown right now, we use an X instead."

Peter: "That makes sense to me! Can you further explain NFR number six anyway? I'm not sure if I completely understand it."

Tamika: "Yes, of course. Basically, what we're saying is that if you are interacting with the phone app, the application should react as quickly as possible. For example, if that X becomes five seconds, then every time you click on something in the application it will take up to five seconds for the system to take you to the next page."

Marla: "What about the last NFR? Can you explain what that one means?"

Tamika: "This one basically means that if you have over 200 people using the system at the same time, then the system will not perform as expected. It will most likely cause delayed response times or could completely be unavailable to users."

Marla: "OK, great—thank you for clarifying! I think I'm good with everything here then."

Peter: "Yes, same here—this makes a lot of sense to me!"

Tamika: "Wonderful! With that, I think we've presented everything, Mrs. Thompson."

Narrator: Mrs. Thompson smiles and directs her attention towards a girl in the corner, motioning for her to come towards the middle of the classroom.

Mrs. Thompson: "Excellent job, Tamika. Now let's hear a progress update from one of our developers. Sophia, would you be willing to give everyone an update on what you, Michelle, and Leah are doing?"

Sophia: "Yes I can! As Tamika said, we reviewed the original list of user needs that were gathered in the initial requirements session. After review, we started building some of the functions, and we are about halfway done with the user needs. I think with this updated information, we should be able to showcase a working product to the group in about two weeks.

Mrs. Evans: "Excellent—that's great to hear. So, after you're done with developing, what happens next?"

Sophia: "Typically when we are done coding something, we will run a couple test scenarios from a system and user perspective. After that, I think it would be good to do a show-and-tell, where we show you all the features that we have built and check to make sure we didn't miss anything. If everyone is good with what we present in the show-and-tell, then we will put the application out in production, which means it will be available for any student to use."

Mrs. Evans: "Great. With that timeline, it sounds like we will be able to get something out to students to use by the end of

March, would you agree?"

Mrs. Thompson: "I think that sounds pretty realistic. Girls, would you agree with that statement?"

Narrator: The girls in the Technology Club nod their heads in agreement.

Mrs. Thompson: "Excellent. Then I say our groups should come back together in about two weeks, and in the meantime, we need a couple volunteers to help with testing."

Peter: "I would be willing to volunteer!"

Marla: "Me too!"

Mrs. Thompson: "Great! Then Tamika and Sophia will connect with you two sometime during the next two weeks to help with testing. With that, I think that's all we have."

Mrs. Evans: "Excellent, this is great progress. Thank you again to everyone in the Technology Club for helping out with this. We will see you in two weeks!"

Narrator: The Technology Club members smile and proceed to leave the classroom. The School Spirit Club stays around for a little while longer and then eventually disbands for the evening.

Chapter Six Guiding and Activity Questions:

1. Review the list of proposed business rules that Tamika and Madeline put together. Do you think there are any business rules that you would add to this list? If yes, what would you add?

2. Review the list of proposed non-functional requirements that Tamika and Madeline put together. Do you think there are any non-functional requirements that you would add to this list? If yes, what would you add?

Chapter Six Key Terms:

- **Business rules**: Definitions or constraints of a business' operations or behavior.

- **Non-Functional Requirements:** Statements that define what a system can or cannot do based on several factors (reliability, performance, maintainability, scalability, usability).

- **X-Factor**: A variable to put in place of a statement when the measure is unknown.

CHAPTER 7 — GET IT INTO PRODUCTION!

After the Technology Club gained approval from Mr. Martinez, and after a few students approved Peter and Marla's prototype, the School Spirit Club and the Technology Club regrouped to discuss next steps and review requirements on a deeper level. The Technology Club is now tasked with building the mobile application. Now that some time has passed, it's time to check in with them and see how they're doing!

Narrator: Time starts to move quickly and several days pass by. As the Technology Club continues to develop out the solution, they eventually become ready for Marla and Peter to assist them with testing the app to make sure it's working correctly. When the time is right, Tamika calls for Marla and Peter to join them after school.

Marla and Peter enter classroom 113 to see the Technology Club working away. Tamika motions for them to come over to her table, where she has two phones placed out for the two of them to interact with.

Tamika: "Thanks again for coming to test a couple scenarios with us. Like we mentioned a few days back, testing what we have built is always a valuable exercise before we finish coding."

Marla: "Of course! We are happy to help even if we aren't exactly sure what we'll be doing. I've never tested anything before."

Tamika: "Totally understandable. The type of testing we are about to do is what we call **User Acceptance Testing**. This essentially means that I want you to act like one of the users you identified in our requirements sessions and see if what you expected to happen in the app is actually happening. For the sake of this exercise, Marla, you will play the role of a student ordering a couple of products and Peter, you will play the role of Mr. Martinez."

Narrator: Tamika then proceeds to hand them each their own phone.

Tamika: "Does that make sense?"

Marla: "Yes, it does now! Is there a particular item you want me to try and buy?"

Tamika: "Yes. How about we do a few scenarios with Marla to start? Peter, we will have you test a couple things in a few minutes. Let's first start with the scenario where you are a first-time user and you don't have a profile yet. Interact with the phone and tell me what's happening."

Narrator: Marla looks down at the phone and starts to interact with it.

Marla: "I am seeing an opportunity to create a new profile. I am being asked to put in some information including my student ID number, name, phone number, and email. After selecting "next," it looks like the application is asking if I want to add any payment information."

Tamika: "OK, great. Go ahead and put in your account info for your Ca$hNow account. After completing that it should take you to the home page."

Narrator: Marla proceeds to put in her information and then indicates that the addition went through.

Tamika: "Excellent. Now let's do the scenario where you want to purchase a specific item but it's out-of-stock. Can you locate the CandyEar Earphones on the home page?"

Narrator: Marla scrolls through the phone until she lands on the earphones.

Marla: "I found the CandyEar Earphones, and I see that I cannot select the item to add to my cart. It also says next to the item that it is out-of-stock."

Tamika: "Excellent! OK, now just pick any item that isn't listed as out-of-stock and go ahead and add it to your cart to buy."

Narrator: Marla selects a couple items and adds them to her electronic shopping cart.

Tamika: "Great, now select the cart icon at the top right of the screen. It should take you to a checkout screen."

Narrator: Marla proceeds to do as Tamika told her and confirms that she sees the checkout screen.

Tamika: "Now you should see that you can edit the quantity of one of your items. Go ahead and change one of the items to wanting two of them. From there, go ahead and proceed to checkout. Because you have your payment information already added, it should take you straight to a confirmation screen."

Marla: "You're correct. I now have a confirmation that my order is complete."

Tamika: "OK, great. Now go check your email to see if you received a confirmation by email as well."

Narrator: Marla pulls out her own phone to check her emails, and sure enough, there is an email identifying the purchase she made.

Tamika: "Excellent, it looks like the expected behavior is correctly coded. Did you see anything that you felt was missing or you didn't like?"

Marla: "No, this looks great to me, and I really like the layout."

Tamika: "Awesome. OK, Peter you're up next. Since it's just Mr. Martinez under the other role, we went ahead and already created a profile for him, so you won't need to create one in this scenario. For your awareness, we are differentiating between the student and faculty profiles through student ID and faculty ID. They are acting as our **unique identifiers**. Because everyone has their own ID; there's no risk for duplicates. Peter, I want you to start by seeing if you received a notification from Marla's order."

Peter: "I see that in my view, there's an inbox icon with a flag over it. After clicking on it, I see an order from Marla for a purchase of two highlighters and one pack of gum."

Marla: "That matches with what I put in my order!"

Tamika: "Great! Now after pretending that you filled the order, tell us what you see."

Peter: "There looks to be an icon that allows me to message the student. After selecting it, it looks like I can identify a date and time for Marla to come to the school store and pick up her goods."

Narrator: Peter proceeds to fill out the date and time stamp.

Peter: "After doing that, it looks like I can also check a box next to the order request that indicates that the order is complete."

Tamika: "Marla, can you confirm if you got an email about your pickup time?"

Marla: "Yep, I got an email saying to come to the school store to-morrow at 12 p.m."

Tamika: "Awesome. Peter anything else you see?"

Peter: "Well, after I selected that the order is complete, the app took me back to the home page and I see a summary of all sales for this month. I can also see the total of $5.00 from Marla's purchase."

Tamika: "Great! Thoughts about the experience?"

Peter: "I really liked it and I feel that Mr. Martinez will really like it, too."

Tamika: "Yes, hopefully he will! With that, our testing is done for now. I realize that I didn't have you two go through every scenario, but we did get to test some of our normal paths, or the most common behaviors you could expect from both user types. We will continue to test on our side, but that's all we need from you two right now."

Marla: Great — I'm glad we could be of help!"

Narrator: Marla and Peter return the phones and say their good-byes as they leave the classroom.

It's a few days later and the Technology Club has completed their development and testing of the mobile app. Mrs. Thompson reaches out to Mrs. Evans, and in their next joint club meeting, the Technology Club facilitates a **show-and-tell** presentation of the app, where they walk the School Spirit Club through all the expected scenarios. Mr. Martinez also comes to the meeting to see the final product.

After a healthy discussion, the School Spirit Club members and Mr. Martinez are very pleased with the results and give the go-ahead for the Technology Club to put the application into **production.** This means that the application will become available to every student for download.

Chapter Seven Guiding and Activity Questions:

1. Work with a partner to write out a user testing scenario for one of the previously recorded user requirements in Chapter 5. Be prepared to share in class.
   a. Example: A student paying with a credit card instead of the Ca$hNow App.

Chapter Seven Key Terms:

- **Production:** Software that is currently ready and available to be used by its defined customers.

- **Show-and-tell**: A ceremony for Agile build teams in which work on a piece of software is shown to the users and/or customers to gather feedback.

- **Unique identifier:** A piece of data that can provide representation to a specific item or person. For example, a social security number is a unique identifier for an American citizen.

- **User Acceptance Testing (U.A.T):** The level of testing where the functionality of the software is validated by a real user to determine if it's working correctly or not

CHAPTER 8
(CONCLUSION) —
THE AFTERMATH

After a successful session of User Acceptance Testing, the mobile application has been built and reviewed with Mr. Martinez and the School Spirit Club members. After all of the positive feedback, the Technology Club puts the application into production.

As we reach the end of our story, let's find out what has resulted from putting the mobile app out for the students of Riverwood Middle School to use.

Narrator: As the school year proceeds further into spring, the school store app becomes widely available for any student to download. Fortunately, no **bugs** are discovered upon implementation. Thanks to the assistance of the school newspaper, morning announcements, and teachers throughout the school, word quickly gets out about the application. At the start, there aren't too many sales, but interest quickly picks up, and before Mr. Martinez knows it, he is filling more orders than he has ever had!

As we reach the end of April, thirty days away from the iconic field trip to Happy Amusement park, the School Spirit Club checks in to see the progress of fundraising sales from the school store. Thanks to their technology solution, they see the following numbers for this year in comparison to the past years:

	Two Years Ago	Last Year	Current Year
School Store	$4,244.50	$3,649.30	$4,458.00
Bake Sale	$1,400.00	$1,601.50	$1,650.40
Book Festival	$1,429.50	$1,281.20	$1,568.60
Total	$7,074.00	$6,523.00	$7,677.00
Comparison to goal	$7,074/$7,860 (90%)	$6,523/$8,320 (79%)	$7,677/$8,530 (90%)

Since the numbers are looking much more favorable and consistent with past years, there is a very high confidence that the

School Spirit Club's fundraising goal will definitely be achieved by the field trip date. Due to the speed of increased sales in the quarter, there is even the possibility that they may exceed their goal this year, which will allow for next year to start with a little extra cushion. Mrs. Evans and the School Spirit Club quickly communicate the formal confirmation of the annual field trip and continue with their logistical planning for the big day.

Before they know it, May 30 arrives and all the 8th graders load onto their buses to head to Happy Amusement Park. Marla and Peter celebrate with their fellow Club members and the Technology Club members on the bus ride, knowing that they are in for an incredibly exciting day!

Chapter Eight Key Terms:

Bug: A mistake or error in a computer program that causes something unexpected to happen (the term **defect** can be used interchangeably).

Afterword

Reader, I'd like to start off by saying thank you for taking the time to read my book. I hope that in finishing this book you have learned a couple new things you can add to your toolkit, and hopefully you have a continued interest in learning more about technology. Below are some additional resources I encourage you to check out if interested.

If you're looking to learn more about Agile and Lean concepts:

- Learn more about the Agile manifesto by visiting https://agilemanifesto.org/. There you can learn how Agile became a major methodology within software development, as well as the principles behind the Agile manifesto.
- Learn more about Lean-Agile software and systems concepts through the Scaled Agile Framework (SAFe) at https://www.scaledagile.com/.
- Learn more about the different cloud computing products and services through Amazon Web Services at https://aws.amazon.com.
- Finally, do your own research!
  - Investigate how Agile became a more accepted way of software development and delivery than Waterfall methodology.
  - Search across various websites to learn more about the system development life cycle.

If you're looking to learn more about how to gather requirements:

- Learn more about how others gather requirements at www.modernanalyst.com
- Learn more about non-functional requirements at https://www.scaledagileframework.com/nonfunctional-requirements/
- Learn more about business rules at https://

www.modernanalyst.com/Resources/Articles/
tabid/115/ID/1164/What-You-Need-to-Know-
About-Business-Rules.aspx
- Check out Google Drawings or LucidChart at
www.lucidchart.com to get access to a free tool to
make your own process maps!

If you're looking to learn more about a career as a business analyst:

- Check out the International Institute of Business Analysis to learn more about other business analysis professionals and key topics in the industry at https://www.iiba.org/

If you're looking to learn more about coding and a career as a developer:

- Learn some basic coding concepts through the following programs:
  ◦ Coding with Kids at www.codingwithkids.com – virtual camps and programs for kids to learn about various coding languages
  ◦ Coding Academy at www.codeacademy.com – go-your-own-pace virtual training for various coding languages
  ◦ Girls Who Code at www.girlswhocode.com – an organization dedicated to closing the gender gap in technology and changing the image of what a programmer looks like and does
  ◦ Humble Bundle at www.humblebundle.com – a virtual store that offers a variety of games and learning modules for kids and adults on various coding and technology concepts

If you're looking to learn about other careers in technology:

- Check out the Project Management Institute to learn more about other project management professionals and key topics in the industry at www.pmi.org

Check out the Scrum Master community to learn more about other Scrum Master professionals and key topics in the industry at https://www.scrumalliance.org/

Glossary

- **Agile**: A key concept in software analysis and development. The ability to move quickly and easily when defining requirements and building a solution
- **Agile build team**: A cross-functional group of people who analyze, define, build, test, and deliver a piece of value quickly to their customers through software. Typically, 6-10 people work within a team including analysts, developers, testers, a product owner, and a Scrum Master.
- **Brainstorming**: The act of coming up with multiple ideas.
- **Budget:** An estimate of money coming in and out for a set period of time.
- **Bug**: A mistake or error in a computer program that causes something unexpected to happen (the term **defect** is also used to describe the same thing).
- **Business analyst**: A person who analyzes and defines business needs to improve business processes, products, and service functions.
- **Business rules**: Definitions of or constraints on a business' operations or behavior.
- **Coding**: The process of writing instructions within a computer program to accomplish a specific task.
- **Cost plan:** A proposed look of potential costs expected in a project.
- **Customer**: A person that buys goods or services from a business.
- **Development**: The process of designing, testing, and implementing a new piece of software.
- **Developer**: A person who builds software.
- **Facilitator**: A person who leads and manages a requirements gathering session with the goal of identifying

user needs and requirements.

- **Fail Fast, Learn Quickly**: The Agile concept of trying an idea without the fear of failing, because if you fail fast you can quickly understand what went wrong and learn from it.
- **Feasible (Feasibility)**: The idea that a solution can be easily accomplished.
- **Five Whys**: An analysis technique that allows a person to explore the cause and effect relationships of a situation to identify an underlying problem.
- **Framework**: A software structure a developer can use as a baseline and then make specific coding changes to reach their programming goal.
- **Fundraising**: The act of seeking financial support for a particular reason.
- **Ideate**: To come up with an idea.
- **Interview**: A discussion with one or multiple people to learn about something.
- **Mission statement:** A brief expression of what an organization's overall goal is, what kind of goods or services the organization offers, and why the organization may exist.
- **Non-functional requirements**: Statements that define what a system can or cannot do based on several factors (reliability, performance, maintainability, scalability, usability).
- **Persona**: A perceived representation of a person's or group of people's characteristics.
- **Problem statement**: A brief statement that defines a challenge faced by a business. It typically is seen as a starting point for coming up with a solution, such as a product or technology vision.
- **Project manager**: A person who is in charge of planning and executing a project.
- **Process map**: A tool that can visually show a step-by-

step map of a current or future state process.

- **Production**: Software that is currently ready and available to be used by its defined customers.
- **Programming language**: A set of rules to tell a computer to perform a set of specific tasks.
- **Prototype**: A quick try at describing a solution based on identified requirements.
- **Quality engineer**: A person who makes sure the software or procedures in place are of the best quality possible.
- **Requirements**: Things that are needed or wanted.
- **Revenue**: Money coming in from an organization's sales of goods or services.
- **Root cause**: The reason why a problem exists.
- **Sample size**: The number of people included in a survey research effort.
- **Scribe**: A person who takes notes during a requirements gathering session with the goal of documenting user needs and requirements.
- **Show-and-tell**: A ceremony for Agile build teams in which work on a piece of software is shown to their users and/or customers to gather feedback.
- **Survey**: To conduct research with any number of individuals to discover and/or validate information.
- **Swimlane**: A visual way in a process map that can show the difference between activities of different users in a process.
- **System analysis**: The process of understanding and defining a process or business function in order to identify needs and goals to create systems and procedures that will provide value to the current state.
- **Testing**: The process of checking quality, performance, and/or reliability of developed software. The terms "quality assurance" and "QA testing" are widely recognized in the software development industry.

- **User**: A person that uses or will use a piece of software that has been developed for their needs.
- **User Acceptance Testing (U.A.T)**: The level of testing where the functionality of the software is validated by a real user to determine if it's working correctly or not
- **User stories**: Brief descriptions of the needs of a user. Used to help communicate requirements in building software.
- **User testing**: The process of validating the functions of a product or service by a real user to determine if it's working correctly or not.
- **V.A.E.R.**: Acronym used to help capture all potential scenarios when gathering requirements. Stands for: View, Add, Edit, Remove.
- **Validate** – To check that something is correct.
- **X-Factor**: A variable put in place of a statement when the measure is unknown.
- **Unique identifier:** A piece of data that can provide representation to a specific item or person. For example, a social security number is a unique identifier for an American citizen.

COMPANION GUIDE

Analyze It!

A fun and easy introduction to software analysis and the information technology industry

by Kristen Elliott

Introduction

Hello, and welcome to the companion guide to **Analyze It!** The purpose of this guide is to provide supplementary information to support the book's key topics and terms. This guide was written to provide further context on what was provided in the text, as well as cover additional topics for learning on your own or teaching in the classroom.

This guide has been written with two key individuals in mind:

1. The student who has read the primary text and is interested in diving deeper into technology concepts, and
2. The teacher looking to integrate the book within their classroom as a lesson plan.

How this guide is organized:

- A summary overview of the problem and solution prompts from the book.
- Recommendations on how to best utilize the book, as well as supplementary information presented as a lesson plan series.
- A breakout of each lesson including:
   - An abstract of the included chapter(s),
   - Key questions to consider in support of the chapter(s), and
   - Additional information and topics for consideration.

I hope that you find this information intriguing and useful for you, whether it is inside or outside a classroom. And again, thank you for taking the time to read. I hope you enjoy!

— Kristen

Problem Prompt:
The School Spirit Club at Riverwood Middle School is currently focused on preparing the annual 8th grade field trip to Happy Amusement Park. The funds for this trip are gathered through various fundraising events throughout the year, as well as from revenue from the school store. Unfortunately, sales from the school store have not been as high as in previous years, and there is a serious risk that the School Spirit Club will not reach their fundraising goal.

Members of the School Spirit Club work together to determine that the root cause of their fundraising challenges is that customer preferences have shifted to using electronic payments rather than cash-based payments, and the school store only accepts cash.

Solution Prompt:
The School Spirit Club members brainstorm potential ideas to solve their identified problem. They eventually agree on the idea of making a mobile application that every student can use to view and purchase items from the school store electronically. They collaborate with the Technology Club to identify user requirements for the application, and gain approval to build the application after presenting a prototype to their key stakeholders (the owner of the school store, Mr. Martinez, and several students within Riverwood Middle School).

The Technology Club develops the application, and after necessary user testing and a show-and-tell experience, the application is out for public use. Students begin to use the app, and the school store bounces back to gain additional revenue, which prevents the annual 8th grade trip from being cancelled.

Lesson Plan Series Proposal

Below is a proposed lesson plan series that can be used in the classroom:

Lesson Number	Reading Text	Key Questions	Supplementary Text
1	Chapter 1 — No Amusement Park Trip? I am not amused!	How do businesses/organizations explain who they are? How do businesses determine what they are trying to achieve and how they measure success? What is a budget and how is it different from a cost plan?	Introduction to the following concepts: - Mission statement - Business objective - Key performance indicator - Budget - Cost plan
2	Chapter 2 — Let's get down to business (and what's wrong with it). Chapter 3 — Problem has been analyzed! Now, what about a solution...?	What is a problem statement? What are different ways we can identify a problem? (Examples: surveys, interviews, root cause analysis) What are the differences between a customer, a user, and a stakeholder? What is a persona? What is brainstorming? What is a prototype? What is design thinking?	Introduction to the following concepts: - Problem statement - Problem analysis - Customer - User - Stakeholder - Persona - Brainstorming - Prototyping - Design thinking
3	Chapter 4 — Welcome, Technology Club!	What is the system development life cycle? What are different software methodologies that are used today? What is Waterfall? What is Agile? How is it different from Waterfall methodology? What is Scrum? What is an Agile build team? Who makes up an Agile build team? What does an Agile build team do during an iteration (sprint)?	Introduction to the following concepts: - System development life cycle (SDLC) - Waterfall - Agile - Scrum - Agile build team - Iteration (Sprint) - Analyst - Developer - Tester - Product owner - Scrum Master - Product backlog - Sprint backlog - Planning meeting - Show-and-tell - Retrospective - Technology consultant - Application owner - Project manager - Portfolio manager

		What are the major types of careers in technology today? (Examples: analysis, development, testing, project management, product management, portfolio management, Scrum Master, application owner)	
4	Chapter 5 — Let's get to the main requirements! Chapter 6 — Check-in time!	What are key ways we can identify user needs? What are key ways we can document user needs?	Introduction to the following concepts: - Requirements elicitation - Facilitator - Scribe - User stories vs. epics vs. features - Business Process Modeling Notation (BPMN) - Unified Modeling Language - Use case diagram - Use case scenarios - Business rules - Non-functional requirements
6	Chapter 7 — Get it into production! Chapter 8 — The aftermath	What is testing? What are different types of testing? What does it mean when we release technology? What happens after a piece of technology is completed?	Introduction to the following concepts: - Testing - Unit testing - Integration testing - System testing - User Acceptance Testing - Release - Software maintenance

A few considerations:

- The lesson plan is organized by chapter(s) and overarching trends. As a result, some lessons may take longer than others to complete.
- The primary text reads like a script and allows the opportunity for a student to read aloud as a specific character.
- At the end of every chapter (in the primary text), there are a couple of activity suggestions that can help supplement the reading.
- The additional topics intended to support the text are presented as guidelines for you to determine what to add into your curriculum. They could either be pre-

sented in lecture format or in more interactive ways through student participation.

Lesson #1 – Business Organization and Strategy Foundations

Reading section: Chapter 1 — No Amusement Park Trip? I am not amused!

Abstract of Chapter 1:

The members of the School Spirit Club meet together to begin planning for the end-of-year 8th grade field trip to Happy Amusement Park. In determining how much money is left for them to fundraise, they discover a major problem: they are further behind than in past years and are at risk of not reaching their goal.

Key questions to consider:

- How do businesses/organizations explain who they are?
- How do businesses determine what they are trying to achieve and how they measure success?
- What is a budget and how is it different from a cost plan?

Supplementary Text:

Mission Statement —

A mission statement is a brief expression of what an organization's overall goal is, what kind of goods or services the organization offers, and why the organization may exist. The value of a mission statement is that it allows a business to define its culture, values, ethics, and overall goals. It reveals *what* a business operates, *how* it operates, and *why* it operates. A mission statement is typically a short paragraph or a single sentence.

Below are examples of mission statements from some well-known companies:
- **Nike:** To bring inspiration and innovation to every athlete in the world

- **Starbucks:** To inspire and nurture the human spirit – one person, one cup, and one neighborhood at a time
- **J.P. Morgan:** To be the best financial services company in the world

Business Objective —

A business objective is a desired outcome that a company aims to achieve. Unlike a goal, which is a broader strategic outcome, a business objective focuses specifically on a measurable step to reach a goal.

When writing a business objective, try following the acronym M.A.C.S.:

- Is it **M**easurable?
- Is it **A**ctionable?
- Is it **C**oncrete?
- Is it **S**pecific?

Below are a couple examples of business objectives:

- Profit maximization: By the end of the first year of operations, X company aims to reach $1 million in revenue.
- Creation of jobs: By end of the third quarter, Y company aims to generate 100 new jobs within their technology department.
- Sales growth: Z company looks to increase overall sales growth of their life insurance product channel by 5% within the next three to five years.

Key Performance Indicator (KPI) —

A key performance indicator is a measure of progress toward a desired result. KPIs can be used to define a measurement in a business objective through either:

- Input attributes (example: the materials used to make a product)
- Output attributes (example: the output quality of the

product made)
- Process attributes (example: efficiency of making a product)
- Outcome attributes (example: customer satisfaction)

KPIs can also be used to focus on:

- Tactical, day-to-day operations in a business
- Project progress and effectiveness
- Risks that can challenge a business
- Human engagement needed to make a business' operations successful

Budget —

A budget is an estimate of money coming in and out for a set period of time. Budgets are typically specified for a future period of time and are often re-evaluated. Anyone or anything that makes and spends money can have a budget (an individual, a group of people, a business, an organization, a government, etc.)

There are two major types of budgets: static budgets and flexible budgets. Static budgets represent estimated money in and out, and items that will remain unchanged over the life of the budget.

Here are a few examples of a static budget:

- *X company decides to replace all of its old computers for its employees over the next five years. They calculate that it will cost them $100,000 for all of their computers, resulting in a static expense schedule of $20,000 per year.*
- *Y company is given a yearly budget of $1 million per year for research and development work.*
- *Z company manages a factory and has fixed expenses for*

rent.

Flexible budgets detail money in or out that has a relational value due to other variables that are occurring.

Here are a few examples of a flexible budget:

- *X company expects a decreased revenue stream this year due to an economic downturn.*
- *Z company manages a factory that has variable expenses for increased labor during the holidays due to increased product demand.*

Cost Plan —

A cost plan is a proposed look at potential costs expected in a project. Cost plans are estimated future costs for a project, which are different from budgets.

Cost plans evolve through the life of a project and are continuously updated as more information becomes available. A budget plays as a variable, however, in the management of a cost plan. For example, if the cost plan exceeds a business' budget, scope of the cost plan may be reduced to accommodate.

References:

Chen, James. "Why Mission Statements Matter." Investopedia. Investopedia, October 20, 2020. https://www.investopedia.com/terms/m/missionstatement.asp.

"Difference between Cost Plan and Budget." Difference between cost plan and budget - Designing Buildings Wiki. Accessed November 5, 2020. https://www.designingbuildings.co.uk/wiki/Difference_between_cost_plan_and_budget.

Ganti, Akhilesh. "Budget Definition." Investopedia. Investopedia, September 15, 2020. https://www.investopedia.com/terms/b/budget.asp.

"What Is a Business Objective? Definition and Meaning." Market Business News, June 9, 2020. https://marketbusinessnews.com/financial-glossary/business-objective-definition-meaning/.

"What Is a Key Performance Indicator (KPI)?" kpi.org. Accessed November 5, 2020. https://kpi.org/KPI-Basics.

Lesson #2 — Core Analysis Concepts, Part 1

Reading sections: Chapter 2 — Let's get down to business (and what's wrong with it).; Chapter 3 — Problem has been analyzed! Now what about a solution...?

Abstract of Chapter 2:

The School Spirit Club identifies the potential root cause of the identified problem in Chapter 1. They interview Mr. Martinez, the owner of the school store, and form a hypothesis that the store has been losing sale opportunities because it is a cash-only operation. They build a survey to ask several students to validate.

Abstract of Chapter 3:

Members of the School Spirit Club survey their friends and validate that their hypothesis is correct. Now knowing the actual problem statement, they brainstorm and come up with several ideas on how to solve the problem. They eventually land on building a mobile app with the Technology Club that will allow students to buy products using an electronic payment method.

Key questions to consider:

- What is a problem statement?
- What are different ways we can identify a problem? (Examples: surveys, interviews, root cause analysis)
- What are the differences between a customer, a user, and a stakeholder?
- What is a persona?
- What is brainstorming?
- What is a prototype?
- What is design thinking?

Supplementary Text

Problem statement —

A problem statement is a brief statement that defines a challenge faced by a business. It is typically seen as a starting point for coming up with a solution, such as a product or technology vision.

Defining a problem statement will allow you/your team to gather ideas to establish features/functions to solve the identified problem.

Think of the following questions when forming a problem statement:

- *What is the actual problem affecting your business?*
- *Who is affected by this problem?*
- *What kind of impact exists because of this problem?*

Problem analysis —

Problem analysis is the act of investigating the cause of an identified problem. In software analysis and development, problem analysis is a critical step in identifying improvements to existing technology, or deciding to build new technology. It is a critical function within the role of an analyst.

There are many different techniques an analyst can use to evaluate a problem, including:

- Interviewing a person (one-on-one or through surveys)
- Conducting a root cause analysis
    - ◦ Note: The primary text identifies the Five Whys as an example of how to perform a root cause analysis.

Customer vs. User vs. Stakeholder —

There are three major types of roles that are the focus of software analysis: the customer, the user, and the stakeholder.

- A customer is a person that buys goods or services from a business.
- A stakeholder is a person or group of people that are actively tied to a business or project and are impacted by the results of decision-making.
- A user is a person that uses (or will use) a piece of software that has been developed for their needs.
- In software analysis and development, a user can also be a business' stakeholder or customer. This depends on the purpose of the technology that is being built and who it is intended for.

Persona —

A persona is a perceived representation of a person's or group of people's characteristics. In software analysis and development, personas are researched and then created to help outline their overall goals, behaviors, pain points, and other helpful information. A persona can be conveyed through a very simple statement or an in-depth analysis.

There are many techniques used to create a persona. A couple examples include:

- Interviewing people that fit within an identified persona through one-on-one discussions or through a survey format.
- Creating an empathy map (a visual aid that helps identify what a person says, thinks, does, and feels in respect to a situation).

Below is an example of an empathy map of a customer interacting with the school store at the beginning of the story before the

School Spirit Club worked to fix the identified problem:

SAYS	THINKS
• "I don't have any cash on me." • "Can you accept other forms of payment?" • "When will you have that back in stock?"	• *This is annoying that I can only pay with cash.* • *I really need this today, not tomorrow.* • *I could just borrow X from a friend today instead of buying a new one.*
DOES	**FEELS**
• Looks around the school store but doesn't purchase anything • Asks a friend to borrow X instead of going to the store	• Frustrated due to lack of flexibility with the store's payment policy

Brainstorming —

Brainstorming is the act of coming up with multiple ideas. As stated in the primary text, brainstorming should be treated as a no-judgement activity where the goal is to come up with as many ideas as possible for a problem. Once a series of ideas has been identified, then the involved group can work through them to determine the desirability, feasibility, and viability of each option.

A few guardrails recommended to follow when brainstorming:

- Brainstorming should not be an individual activity; involving a group of people allows opportunities for broader thinking.
- Everyone involved needs to participate; one person should not dominate the conversation.
- In group brainstorming, it is recommended to have a facilitator to help move the conversation along, as well as a scribe to document all ideas (see lesson #4 for more information on facilitator and scribe roles).

- No one should judge an initial idea.
- Brainstorming should have a time limit in order to prevent burnout, and to prevent "rabbit hole" conversations from occurring.

Prototype —

A prototype is a quick try at describing a solution based on identified requirements. In software analysis, it's used as a non-working mock-up of a real system to show to users and stakeholders in order to validate user requirements and discover any missing requirements.

Prototypes are typically either low-technology or high-technology. A low-technology prototype is a very cheap and direct mock-up to demonstrate value quickly. It's used most often in analysis as a validation tool.

Here is an example of a low-tech prototype: Let's use the scenario of a basic checkout page. In this prototype we want to showcase the functionality that a customer can do the following:

- View a summary of their order
- Select to change the quantity of any item in their order
- Add their shipping and billing address
- Add their payment information
- Select to submit their order for processing

Below is an easy mock-up of what that checkout summary page would look like:

A high-technology prototype is a more invested mock-up that, down the road, can be further refined and potentially become the real technology solution. An example of a high-technology prototype would be a piece of coded logic to demonstrate functionality for an identified business process.

Design thinking —

Design thinking is a mindset used in software analysis and development that tackles human-centric, complex problems. The mindset focuses on identifying who you're solving for, what their needs are, and how you will solve for them.

Design thinking is tackled in five stages:

- **Empathizing**: Understanding the human needs involved
- **Defining**: Re-framing and defining the problem in

human-centric ways

- **Ideating**: Creating many ideas in brainstorming sessions
- **Prototyping**: Creating an experience for your customer that you are able to test
- **Testing**: Gathering feedback and reactions to make sure you are focused on the right problem, and that you have a viable solution for that problem

The important thing to remember is that design thinking is a non-linear process. Often, an analyst using design thinking will move between stages depending on the progression of a need.

References:

"4 Examples of Problem Analysis." Simplicable, 2020. https://simplicable.com/new/problem-analysis.

Admin, IDEO U. "What Is Design Thinking?" IDEO U. IDEO U, June 26, 2020. https://www.ideou.com/blogs/inspiration/what-is-design-thinking.

Bland, David. "What Is an Empathy Map?" SolutionsIQ, April 10, 2019. https://www.solutionsiq.com/resource/blog-post/what-is-an-empathy-map/.

Bloomenthal, Andrew. "Cashing in on Customers." Investopedia. Investopedia, September 24, 2020. https://www.investopedia.com/terms/c/customer.asp.

Dam, Rikke Friis, and Teo Yu Siang. "What Is Design Thinking and Why Is It So Popular?" The Interaction Design Foundation, 2019. https://www.interaction-design.org/literature/article/what-is-design-thinking-and-why-is-it-so-popular.

"End User." End User Definition. Accessed November 5, 2020. https://techterms.com/definition/enduser.

Famuyide, Stephanie. "What Is a Problem Statement?" Business Analyst Learnings, August 17, 2020. https://businessanalystlearnings.com/ba-techniques/.

GeeksforGeeks. "Software Engineering: Prototyping Model." GeeksforGeeks, October 19, 2020. https://www.geeksforgeeks.org/software-engineering-prototyping-model/.

Gray, Dave, Sunni Brown, and James Macanufo. *Gamestorming: a Playbook for Innovators, Rulebreakers, and Changemakers.* Sebastopol: O'Reilly Media, Inc., USA, 2010.

Gray, Dave. "Updated Empathy Map Canvas." Medium. The XPLANE Collection, July 21, 2018. https://medium.com/the-xplane-collection/updated-empathy-map-canvas-46df22df3c8a.

McCready, Ryan. "20+ User Persona Examples, Templates and Tips For Targeted Decision-Making." Venngage, August 6, 2020. https://venngage.com/blog/user-persona-examples/.

Smith, L.W. "Stakeholder Analysis: a Pivotal Practice of Successful Projects." *Project Management Institute Annual Seminars & Symposium.* Paper presented at the Project Management Institute Annual Seminars & Symposium, 2000.

"Using the Brainstorming Technique in Business Analysis." Using the Brainstorming Technique in Business Analysis > Business Analyst Community & Resources | Modern Analyst. Accessed November 5, 2020. https://www.modernanalyst.com/Resources/Articles/tabid/115/ID/2067/Using-the-Brainstorming-Technique-in-Business-Analysis.aspx.

World Leaders in Research-Based User Experience. "Empathy Mapping: The First Step in Design Thinking." Nielsen Norman Group, 2020. https://www.nngroup.com/articles/empathy-mapping/.

Lesson #3 — Introduction to Agile Concepts and Technology Careers

Reading section: Chapter 4 — Welcome, Technology Club!

Abstract of Chapter 4:

The School Spirit Club meets with the Technology Club for the first time. They learn about the Club's purpose and the different roles each of the students play in the group. The roles of the Technology Club students correspond with potential technology careers for them when they are older. The members of the School Spirit Club discuss their problem statement and proposed solution with the Technology Club. They all agree to have a requirements gathering session.

Key questions to consider:

- *What is the System Development Life Cycle?*
- *What are different software methodologies that are used today?*
  - *What is Waterfall?*
  - *What is Agile? How is it different from Waterfall methodology?*
  - *What is scrum?*
    - *What is an Agile build team?*
    - *Who makes up an Agile build team?*
    - *What does an Agile build team do during an iteration (sprint)?*
- *What are the major types of careers in technology today? (Examples: analysis, development, testing, project management, product management, portfolio management, Scrum Master, application owner)*

Supplementary Text

System Development Life Cycle —

The **System Development Life Cycle (S.D.L.C.)** is a conceptual model that demonstrates the stages involved in analyzing, developing, and delivering software.

The general stages within S.D.L.C. are:

- **Analysis**: Evaluating the existing system or evaluating needs for a new system
- **Design**: Laying out proposed design specifications for a system including hardware, operating system requirements, programming, security considerations, etc.
- **Development**: Coding the system to turn analysis into reality
- **Testing**: Validating that the added code within development is working correctly per identified user needs
- **Deployment**: Putting the system into production, or essentially making the system available for its users to use the product
- **Maintenance**: Making any adjustments after the system is deployed

Software frameworks and mindsets —

There are many software methodologies that are used in practice today. Three of the major frameworks are:

1. Waterfall methodology

Waterfall is a more traditional approach to software analysis and development. This methodology focuses on a linear approach in which you build upon a sequence of events. You begin by gathering and documenting requirements, then move on to designing, developing, performing User Acceptance Testing, and finally delivering a finished product.

As technology becomes more prevalent, however, there is a need to deliver solutions more quickly to customers. As a result, Waterfall is becoming less used in practice because it takes so long to deliver software.

2. Agile methodology

The adjective "agile" is the ability to move quickly and easily when defining requirements and building a solution. Agile methodology is a key concept in software analysis and development and acts as an umbrella term for a set of frameworks and practices. It also acts as a mindset; when you face uncertain challenges, try something quickly, get feedback, and adjust accordingly.

Agile became prevalent in software analysis and development in the early 2000s with the creation of the Agile Manifesto. The Agile Manifesto is a declaration that focuses on the mindset of Agile. It was written in 2001 alongside the birth of Agile software development practices.

The Manifesto focuses on four principles:

1. Individuals and interactions over processes and tools
2. Working software over comprehensive documentation
3. Customer collaboration over contract negotiation
4. Responding to change over following a plan

In these declarations, the items on the left of each statement are valued more than the items on the right.

The Agile methodology in practice focuses on breaking software analysis and development into smaller chunks, which are called iterations or sprints (these terms are interchangeable). An iteration (or sprint) is usually two to four weeks of dedicated analysis, development, and delivery activities. Delivering in an iterative approach allows value to be delivered faster to customers, as well as the ability to make changes more easily when requested by the customer.

3. Scrum

Scrum is a framework that resides under the umbrella of the Agile methodology. It is a more dedicated focus on how to address complex problems through team collaboration, flexibility, and big visible culture.

Scrum follows three thoughts:

1. Scrum is lightweight
2. Scrum is simple to understand
3. Scrum is difficult to master

Typically, Agile build teams (also called scrum teams or cross-functional teams) work together to enact the scrum framework. An Agile build team is a group of people who analyze, define, build, test, and deliver a piece of value quickly to their customers through software. The typical size of an agile build team is 6-10 people.

Below are specific roles that are identified within an Agile build team:

Product owner —

The product owner is the person on the team that is responsible for maximizing the value of work that is done from the team. Their responsibility is to manage the product backlog, which is a list of all potential software work the team may complete.

The product owner prioritizes and pulls items for the team to work on based on whether or not the team can actually do the work, as well as if the customer wants that work delivered sooner than other pieces of work.

Scrum Master —

The Scrum Master is the person on the team that is responsible for supporting the scrum framework. They often act as the "mom" of the team, which means they make sure certain ceremonies are completed per iteration such as:

- Iteration (or sprint) planning meeting: An activity that happens on the first day of an iteration where the team members determine which items are being pulled out of the product backlog and into the bucket (or sprint backlog) to work on for the iteration (two to four weeks).
- Show-and-tell: An activity at the end of the iteration where the team showcases a piece of software built for their users, customers, and/or stakeholders in aims to gather feedback.
- Retrospective: An activity at the end of the iteration where the team discusses internally what went well, as well as what could be improved upon for the next iteration.

The Scrum Master also removes any challenges that may be coming from outside stakeholders or other parties. This is to prevent the other members on the team from getting distracted.

Scrum individuals —

These individuals are the remaining members of an Agile build team. They work together to actually complete the work prioritized by the product owner.

An individual can act as:

- An **analyst**: The person who analyzes and defines user needs to identify what needs to be developed.

- A **developer**: The person who actually builds the software through coding.
- A **tester**: The person who checks quality, performance, and/or reliability of the developed software.

Often, the individuals listed above can play any of these roles; it depends on the needs during the iteration. These individuals will often work together in a close-knit environment to expedite coding and completion of identified work. These individuals will also typically meet every day in a daily standup meeting, which allows them to discuss what each person is currently working on and what challenges they may be facing.

Other Technology Roles

There are other technology roles that do not reside within an Agile build team. A few to mention:

Technology consultant —

A technology consultant is an individual that works closely with a business customer to help them transform the way they see and use technology. This individual often sits in a "planning" function, which allows them to more deeply understand their customer's needs and objectives and determine how technology may enable their needs.

The functions of a technology consultant often range depending on the need. A few of those functions include:

- Performing capability analysis on a business function
- Doing industry trend research to provide a proactive recommendation to a business client on investing money into a piece of technology
- Determining a "buy vs. build" scenario for a piece of technology (Should the business build the software internally or purchase software externally for out-of-the-box use?)

Application owner —

An application owner is the individual who is responsible for the quality, functioning, and services of a particular piece of technology (i.e., application). They act as the custodian of the application including the data that resides within the application. This individual will work to make sure the application is running smoothly, as well as champion any fixes or enhancements that need to be made.

Project manager —

A project manager is the individual who works to deliver a piece of technology through planning and execution of a timeline.

This individual plays several functions including:

- Building a project team
- Building a project plan with defined scope and timeline parameters
- Communicating the goals of the project to the team
- Communicating updates, risks, and issues identified throughout the project to the team and its stakeholders
- Managing expectations and tasks amongst the project team

The project manager has to wear several hats to be successful in their role. They must have the necessary technical acumen to understand the scope and requirements of the project, while also being able to lead a cross-functional group of people with no direct authority.

Portfolio manager —

A portfolio manager is the individual who manages one or multiple investment portfolios based on a project or group of projects. This individual will measure estimated versus actual spend of money for a software project to help determine if the project is meeting its return on investment (R.O.I.). Further, they will partner closely with the project manager to help prioritize projects when necessary.

References:

Bridges, Jennifer. "Key Portfolio Manager Responsibilities." ProjectManager.com. ProjectManager.com, July 3, 2020. https://www.projectmanager.com/training/what-do-portfolio-managers-do.

Lotz, Mary. "Waterfall vs. Agile: Which Methodology Is Right for Your Project?" Segue Technologies, November 20, 2018. https://www.seguetech.com/waterfall-vs-agile-methodology/.

Manifesto for Agile Software Development, 2001. https://agilemanifesto.org/.

PricewaterhouseCoopers. "Technology Consultants: What Do They Do? And How 'Tech' Do You Need to Be?" PwC, 2019. https://www.pwc.com.au/careers/blog/technology-consultants.html.

Project-Management.com. "Project Manager Roles and Responsibilities for Software Projects." Project, October 16, 2018. https://project-management.com/project-manager-roles-responsibilities-software-projects/.

Rouse, Margaret. "What Is Systems Development Life Cycle? - Definition from WhatIs.com." SearchSoftwareQuality. TechTarget, June 21, 2019. https://searchsoftwarequality.techtarget.com/definition/systems-development-life-cycle.

"The Scrum Framework Poster." Scrum.org, 2019. https://www.scrum.org/resources/scrum-framework-poster.

"Technology Consulting Services." Accenture, 2020. https://www.accenture.com/us-en/services/consulting/technology-consulting.

University, Chapman. "Application Owner Roles and Responsibilities." Chapman University Information Systems, 2020. https://www.chapman.edu/campus-services/information-systems/_files/security/3rd-Party-Application-Standards-for-User-Administration.pdf.

"What Is a Product Owner?" Scrum.org, 2020. https://www.scrum.org/resources/what-is-a-product-owner.

"What Is a Scrum Development Team?" Scrum.org, 2020. https://www.scrum.org/resources/what-is-a-scrum-development-team.

"What Is a Scrum Master?" Scrum.org, 2019. https://www.scrum.org/resources/what-is-a-scrum-master.

"What Is Agile Software Development?" Agile Alliance, January 16, 2020. https://www.agilealliance.org/agile101/.

"What Is Scrum?" Scrum.org, 2018. https://www.scrum.org/resources/what-is-scrum.

Lesson #4 — Core Analysis Concepts, Part 2

Reading sections: Chapter 5 — Let's get to the main requirements!; Chapter 6 — Check-in Time!

Abstract of Chapter 5:

Marla and Peter from the School Spirit Club meet with Tamika and Madeline from the Technology Club and have their requirements gathering session. During their time together they identify the list of user needs for two personas (student; Mr. Martinez), as well as plot out a future state process flow diagram.

Abstract of Chapter 6:

Marla and Peter create a prototype based off of initial requirements and showcase it to Mr. Martinez and several members of the School Spirit Club. The prototype is received positively, and the two clubs continue to move forward with building the mobile app. The groups regather a few days later and validate a couple of questions, as well as review current business rules and non-functional requirements.

Key questions to consider:

- *What are key ways we can identify user needs?*
- *What are key ways we can document user needs?*

Supplementary Text

Requirements elicitation —

Requirements elicitation is the act of discovering and gathering business requirements to identify business needs, risks, and assumptions associated with any given initiative. An analyst will typically manage requirements elicitation sessions.

Two major roles that an analyst may play during an elicitation session include:

1. Facilitator
   - The person who leads and manages a require-

ments elicitation session with the goal of identifying user needs and requirements

2. Scribe

  ○ The person who takes notes during a requirements elicitation session with the goal of documenting user needs and requirements

There are many different techniques to elicit requirements. A few to mention:

- Interviewing a person or group of people
- Conducting a survey
- Performing document analysis by gathering and reviewing all existing documentation that may be related to the business objective
- Observing a user through their physical environment (i.e., job shadowing)

User stories vs. Epics vs. Features —

Once business needs are gathered, an analyst will often document the needs in a certain way. Below are three key ways business needs can be identified:

User stories —

User stories are short statements written from the perspective of a user. This type of requirement allows the reader to view how a user would want to work with an end solution.

When writing a user story, try following the acronym S.M.A.R.T.:

- Is it **S**pecific? (Does the user story identify specifically what you want to accomplish?)
- Is it **M**easurable? (Is there a metric you can use to determine if you have met your goal?)
- Is it **A**chievable? (Is it able to be accomplished easily?)
- Is it **R**elevant? (Does it align to your broader business

goals?)

- Is it **T**ime-bound? (Can it be completed in a short period of time (e.g., one sprint)?)

An example of a user story is, *"As a user, I want to be able to be alerted when I receive an email so that I know when my inbox has new messages."*

Epics —

Epics are essentially larger pieces of work that can be broken into smaller tasks. They are typically broken into user stories. Writing epics allows an analyst to approach a macro-view of user-based functionality, which can then be refined further by breaking them down into more detailed requirements. An example of an epic is, *"Sending an email."*

Features —

Features are pieces of requirements that describe a certain type of functionality. Features can develop into multiple user stories. An example of a feature is, *"Draft messaging."*

Business Processing Modeling Notation (B.P.M.N.) —

Business Processing Modeling Notation (B.P.M.N.) is a modeling tool that is designed to visualize business processes. The value of creating process flow documentation allows a person to easily understand a key business process, which can create further collaboration to define needs for a potential technology solution. Analysts use B.P.M.N. as a standard way to create process flows (current state or future state).

B.P.M.N. is comprised of six major elements:

- **Events**: Triggers that start, change, or finish a process
  - Example of an event: Credit card bill is due in three days
- **Activities**: Tasks that are performed by a person or a system; the task describes what the person or system

is doing

- Example of an activity: Customer logs into their bank profile
- **Gateways**: Decision points that can adjust the flow of events based on certain conditions
    - Example of a gateway: Did the customer put in their correct login information? (Yes/No)
- **Connectors**: Ways to connect your flow objects (events, activities, and gateways) together
    - A connector is typically shown as a straight line with an arrow (known as a sequence flow)
    - A connector can also show transmission of a message (message flow) or an association of an artifact to a flow object (association)
- **Pools**: The frame around a process flow which represents major participants in a process
    - Although there is typically just one pool, there can be multiple pools in a process flow (example: a different company is involved in your process flow)
- **Swimlanes**: All the participants and systems involved in a pool; each role has their own horizontal row where their flow objects are placed

Following is an example of a B.P.M.N. diagram. Let's use the scenario of someone wanting to order a pizza for delivery. In this diagram, we are looking to demonstrate the following:

- The customer realizes that they're hungry.
- The customer goes to their food delivery application.
- The customer enters their food order details and submits.
- The line cook at the restaurant picks up the food order.
- The line cook prepares the meal and indicates it's ready for pickup.

- The driver takes the meal and heads to the customer's house.
- The driver delivers the pizza to the customer.
- The customer eats the pizza and is happy!

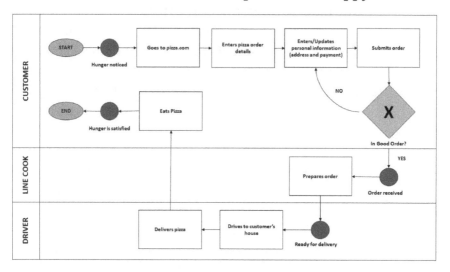

Unified Modeling Language (U.M.L.) —

Unified Modeling Language (U.M.L.) is a standard modeling language that is designed to help technology analysts and developers visualize, specify, and document aspects of software functionality. U.M.L. diagrams help individuals communicate and validate architectural designs of a system. There are multiple types of diagrams that serve a specific purpose. To highlight a couple:

Use case diagram —

A use case diagram is a visual aid that describes at a high level the expected behavior of end users interacting with a system. The expected behavior that a user has with a system is called a use case. Use cases can be further described as use case scenarios. They are not visually shown on a use case diagram, but rather in a different way of documentation.

Use case scenarios are documented in a table format, following a cause-effect relationship. The "cause" side is the user doing something to the system; the "effect" side is the system responding to what the user did.

Here is an example of a use case diagram for a basic ordering system:

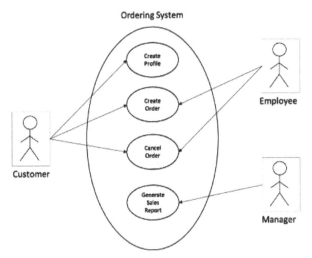

In this example, you see three actors interacting with the ordering system: the customer, the employee, and the manager. The circles inside of the ordering system each represent a use case scenario. The arrows between the actors and the use case scenarios represent who is involved in which scenario.

Let's detail out a use case scenario listed above using a table-based format, where the left side of the table represents anything the actor is doing to the system and the right side of the table represents what the system is doing in response. This is referred to as a stimulus-response approach, or more generically a cause-effect approach:

Actor Action	System Response
<<Step 1>>	<<Step 2>>

Taking the "create order" use case scenario, let's break it out:

Actor Action	System Response
1. Customer searches for item	2. System presents details of item
3. Customer selects item to add to order	4. System adds item to customer's order
5. Customer indicates that they want to proceed with their order	6. System prompts them to add shipping address, billing address, and payment information
7. Customer enters necessary information (shipping address, billing address, payment information)	8. System validates entered information
9. Customer selects to submit order	10. System processes order and returns a confirmation code and delivery date
	11. System sends order information to employee to complete <<END>>

A couple important items to note:

1. What you just read is defined as the normal path. This is where nothing out of the ordinary is happening and as result, the system is reacting as expected. There are often times where certain steps in a use case scenario prompt an alternative scenario that is worth detailing out.

   a. In this example, take a look at step #8. What would happen if the customer accidently mistyped their credit card number? This would cause a new alternative pathway to happen, which could return back to the normal path if mitigated or result in a completely different ending.

2. When writing and reading a use case scenario, you need to make sure you explicitly define your bookends, which are called pre-conditions and post-conditions. A pre-condition is essentially what the world needs to be in order for this scenario to start, whereas a post-condition is what the world will be once the scenario has finished.

   a. In this example, a correct pre-condition would be that the customer has navigated to the ordering system to begin an order and most likely already has a customer profile. A post-condition for this scenario would be that the customer has received a confirmation number and a delivery date for their completed order.

Business rules —

Business rules are definitions or constraints of a business' operations or behavior. A business rule helps an analyst specify guidance or restrictions for a business, which promotes a logical way of thinking when writing requirements.

An example of a business rule is, *"A customer cannot apply for a credit card if they have a credit score less than 500."* Refer to the primary text for more examples of business rules.

Non-functional requirements (NFRs) —

Non-functional requirements (NFRs) are system requirements that define system characteristics. Analysts write NFRs to help identify what a system can or cannot do, which helps them understand the usability and effectiveness of the system. NFRs expand across many different categories including reliability, performance, maintainability, and usability.

An example of an NFR is, "*The system can support up to 2,000 participants.*" Refer to the primary text for more examples of NFRs.

References:

BPMN Specification - Business Process Model and Notation, 2019. http://www.bpmn.org/.

Britsch, Marcel. "The Basics: Epics, Stories, Themes & Features." Medium. The Digital Business Analyst, April 23, 2019. https://thedigitalbusinessanalyst.co.uk/epics-stories-themes-and-features-4637712cff5c.

Leffingwell, Dean. "Nonfunctional Requirements." Scaled Agile Framework, June 30, 2020. https://www.scaledagileframework.com/nonfunctional-requirements/.

Lotz, Mary. "Waterfall vs. Agile: Which Methodology Is Right for Your Project?" Segue Technologies, November 20, 2018. https://www.seguetech.com/waterfall-vs-agile-methodology/.

Masters, Morgan. "An Overview of Requirements Elicitation." Modern Analyst, 2019. https://www.modernanalyst.com/Resources/Articles/tabid/115/ID/1427/An-Overview-of-Requirements-Elicitation.aspx.

Rehkopf, Max. "Epics, Stories, Themes, and Initiatives." Atlassian, 2020. https://www.atlassian.com/agile/project-management/epics-stories-themes.

Ross, Ronald. "What You Need to Know About Business Rules." What You Need to Know About Business Rules > Business Analyst Community & Resources | Modern Analyst, 2020. https://www.modernanalyst.com/Resources/Articles/tabid/115/ID/1164/What-You-Need-to-Know-About-Business-Rules.aspx.

"What Is Business Process Modeling Notation." Lucidchart, 2020. https://www.lucidchart.com/pages/bpmn.

"What Is Unified Modeling Language (UML)? ." Visual Paradigm, 2019. https://www.visual-paradigm.com/

guide/uml-unified-modeling-language/what-is-uml/.

"What Is Use Case Diagram?" Visual Paradigm, 2020. https://www.visual-paradigm.com/guide/uml-unified-modeling-language/what-is-use-case-diagram/.

"Write SMART Goals & INVEST for User Stories." Visual Paradigm, 2020. https://www.visual-paradigm.com/scrum/write-user-story-smart-goals/.

Lesson #5 — Develop, Test, and Deploy

Reading sections: Chapter 7 — Get it into production!; Chapter 8 — The aftermath

Abstract of chapter 7:

The Technology Club is done with building the app and is ready for User Acceptance Testing. Marla tests the main scenarios to make sure the app is working appropriately. She identifies an issue and the Technology Club members fix it. Once done, the Technology Club puts the mobile app into production and does a show-and-tell with the entire School Spirit Club.

Abstract of chapter 8:

The mobile app is now able to be downloaded. After necessary marketing and communications, students begin downloading and using the application. As time progresses closer to May, the School Spirit Club reflects on the positive impact the solution had for the school store. The school store's revenue has increased exponentially, and the School Spirit Club is now on track to reach its fundraising goal. The School Spirit Club has saved the 8th grade field trip! All of the 8th graders, including Marla and Peter, enjoy the field trip once the day arrives.

Key questions to consider

- *What is testing? What are different types of testing?*
- *What does it mean when we release technology?*
- *What happens after a piece of technology is completed?*

Supplementary Text

Testing —

Testing is the process of checking quality, performance, and/or reliability of developed software before putting it into production. Testing allows us to answer the question, *"Is all the functionality of the application, including its inputs and outputs, working as expected?"*

There are different types of testing. A few examples are listed below:

Unit testing —

Unit testing is the level of testing where individual components or parts of a software are tested to validate that each unit is performing as designed. This type of testing is typically completed prior to integration testing

Integration testing —

Integration testing is the level of testing where individual parts of software are combined and tested as a group to identify any faults in the integration between the units. It helps developers identify and expose any defects prior to putting the software into production. This type of testing is typically completed prior to system testing.

System testing —

System testing is the level of testing where the end-to-end software specifications are tested and evaluated in order to determine that the software product is completely integrated. This type of testing is typically completed prior to User Acceptance Testing.

User Acceptance Testing —

User Acceptance Testing (U.A.T.) is the level of testing where the functionality of the software is tested by a real user to determine if it's working correctly or not. The value in doing User Acceptance Testing is that by validating that the expected functionality is working, it's simultaneously reducing time and costs and increasing customer satisfaction when the software is put into production.

Once U.A.T. is complete, the software is typically ready to be released, which means that the final version of the software is ready to be made available to its users (private or public). After the software has been delivered to its customer(s), software maintenance will occur.

Software maintenance can range from modifying or updating the software post-delivery, to correcting any faults found post-release, to making any enhancements to improve performance of the software. The only consistency is that software maintenance occurs over the lifetime of the deployed technology, as software is a continuously living and changing piece of technology.

References:

GeeksforGeeks. "Software Engineering: Software Maintenance." GeeksforGeeks, October 11, 2018. https://www.geeksforgeeks.org/software-engineering-software-maintenance/.

Guru 99. "What Is System Testing? Types & Definition with Example." Guru99, 2019. https://www.guru99.com/system-testing.html.

Rouse, Margaret. "What Is Release? - Definition from WhatIs.com." SearchSoftwareQuality. TechTarget, March 31, 2008. https://searchsoftwarequality.techtarget.com/definition/release.

Setter, Matthew. "What Is User Acceptance Testing (UAT Testing)?" Usersnap, August 26, 2020. https://usersnap.com/blog/user-acceptance-testing-right/.

Stf. "Integration Testing." SOFTWARE TESTING Fundamentals, September 13, 2020. http://softwaretestingfundamentals.com/integration-testing/.

———. "Unit Testing." SOFTWARE TESTING Fundamentals, September 13, 2020. http://softwaretestingfundamentals.com/unit-testing/.

ACKNOWLEDGEMENT

Creating a book is not achieved alone and there are several individuals I'd like to thank for their help. This has been an extremely rewarding experience and I could not have done it without my support team.

To start, I'm extremely thankful for my Mom and Dad. Thank you for always encouraging me to never set limits on myself and establishing my love for learning. I will always be eternally grateful for your love and support.

To my husband, Ted Elliott, who supported me while writing and preparing this book for publication. Thank you, Ted, for being an awesome cheerleader in this crazy life.

A very special thank you to Molly Becker, Matthew Fearrington, and Kristin Gramza, for your collaboration to make this dream a reality. I'm forever indebted to Molly for her editorial help, keen insight, and writing craft to make this story resonate the best possible for my readers. To Matt – thank you for the visually vibrant book cover design that has set the tone for anyone who's interested in reading this book. And to Kristin – thank you for your tireless efforts to get this published book off the ground and into the hands of so many people.

To Melanie Kolp – thank you for being the first leader to mentor and sponsor me when I first started as an

IT communications intern. You introduced me to the software analysis industry and opened so many doors for me to further my career. Thank you for giving me that chance!

To Tom Bihari – thank you for your leadership and encouragement to introduce me to the opportunities of teaching. Being able to teach software analysis to students gave me the confidence to write this book!

To Erin, Jillian, Josh, and Lucas – Thank you for taking the time to read the early drafts of this story. You provided me some very helpful feedback that helped me shape and finalize the content taught in this book.

To my many mentors and sponsors over the years (Jenny, Stacey, Rodney, John, Brian, Gina, Paula, Erin, Noel, Vernon, Mike, Jay, Colleen, Dara, Chris, Mark, Tracie, and many more!)

– thank you so much for your coaching and feedback to help me establish and grow my career. You gave me invaluable experience that helped me breathe life into this book for others to learn from.

And finally, to my twin newborns, Teddy and Ellie. Thank you for coming into my life and making me the happiest mom ever. I wrote this book in the hopes that one day you'll love to learn as much as I do. Also, I wrote this while I was pregnant with you two, so whenever the day comes and you try to avoid doing homework, I plan to use the card "I wrote a book while making you! What's your excuse?" :)

ABOUT THE AUTHOR

Kristen V Elliott

Kristen Elliott is an author, businesswoman, and educator with a background of various analysis and consulting positions. She currently serves as a technology consultant for a Fortune 100 company and teaches software analysis principles at the undergraduate level.

An ambassador of STEAM, Kristen focuses on the advocacy of others to learn more about software analysis and how the power of the arts fuel creativity, critical thinking, and collaboration. She aims to support that mission through teaching, writing, and speaking about various technology concepts and about the power of the arts in a simple and fun way in hopes of others to become empowered to learn more themselves.

She received her MBA at Capital University with a focus in leadership. She also holds two Bachelor degrees (Music and Psychology) from The Ohio State University.

Kristen resides in Columbus, OH with her husband and two children. In her free time, she acts as a freelance violinist and composer. She has performed as a solo act and with multiple local musical groups as a folk, rock, and looper violinist. She has also composed and released two original albums (under the group name "Elliott Collective") and records professional studio strings for several musicians and groups in Ohio.

Made in USA - Kendallville, IN
30736_9781736338216
06.06.2023 1342